road to freedom

Photographs of the Civil Rights Movement 1956–1968

Julian Cox

Introduction by
Charles Johnson

Afterword by
John Lewis

High Museum of Art, Atlanta

For their generous support of the exhibition, we thank:

Sandra Anderson Baccus

The Atlanta Foundation

The Robert Mapplethorpe Foundation

Toyota

National Endowment for the Arts, which believes that a great nation deserves great art

The exhibition *Road to Freedom: Photographs of the Civil Rights Movement, 1956–1968* is organized by the High Museum of Art.

High Museum of Art, Atlanta
June 7–October 5, 2008

The International Gallery
S. Dillon Ripley Center
Smithsonian Institution, Washington, D.C.
November 8, 2008–March 9, 2009

Library of Congress Cataloging-in-Publication Data
Cox, Julian.
    Road to freedom: photographs of the civil rights movement, 1956–1968 / Julian Cox; introduction by Charles Johnson; afterword by John Lewis.
        p. cm.
    Photographs from an exhibition held at the High Museum of Art, Atlanta, June 7–Oct. 5, 2008 and the International Gallery, S. Dillon Ripley Center, Smithsonian Institution, Washington, D.C., Nov. 8, 2008–Mar. 9, 2009.
    Includes bibliographical references.
    ISBN 978-1-932543-23-0 (hardcover: alk. paper)
    ISBN 978-1-932543-21-6 (softcover: alk. paper)
    1. African Americans—Civil rights—History—20th century—Pictorial works—Exhibitions.
2. Civil rights movements—United States—History—20th century—Pictorial works—Exhibitions.
3. Civil rights movements—Southern States—History—20th century—Pictorial works—Exhibitions. 4. United States—Race relations—History—20th century—Pictorial works—Exhibitions. 5. Southern States—Race relations—History—20th century—Pictorial works—Exhibitions. I. High Museum of Art. II. Title.
E185.61.C875 2008
779.42—dc22   2008008856

Published by High Museum of Art, Atlanta

Distributed by University of Washington Press
P.O. Box 50096
Seattle, WA 98145-5096
www.washington.edu/uwpress

Frontispiece: James Karales (American, 1930–2002), *Selma to Montgomery March, Alabama* (detail), 1965, 12½ × 16½ inches (31.8 × 41.9 cm), High Museum of Art, 2007.264. Purchase with funds from Sandra Anderson Baccus in loving memory of Lloyd T. Baccus, M.D.

Title page: Dennis Brack (American, active 1940s–1970s), *Garbagemen's Parade, Memphis, Tennessee* (detail), 1968, gelatin silver print, 9⅝ × 7⁹⁄₁₆ inches (24.4 × 19.2 cm), High Museum of Art, 2007.250. Purchase with funds from Jess and Sherri Crawford in honor of John Lewis

Page 12: Bob Adelman, *Box in Frank Robinson's CORE Voter Registration Office, Sumter, South Carolina*, 1962, detail, plate 44

Page 18: Unknown photographer, *James Forman and John Lewis—Police Mugshots*, gelatin silver prints, 3¾ × 5¹⁄₁₆ inches (9.5 × 12.9 cm), Collection of Emory University, Manuscript, Archives and Rare Book Library

Edited by Kelly Morris,
with Heather Medlock and Rachel Bohan
Catalogue design by Jeff Wincapaw,
with assistance by Tina Kim
Proofread by Jessica Eber
Typeset by Maggie Lee
Color separations by iocolor, Seattle
Produced by Marquand Books, Inc., Seattle
    www.marquand.com
Printed and bound in Singapore
by CS Graphics Pte., Ltd.

Contents

6

Director's Foreword

Michael E. Shapiro

8

Preface and Acknowledgments

Julian Cox

13

Introduction

Charles Johnson

19

Bearing Witness: Photography and the Civil Rights Movement

Julian Cox

48

Plates

146

Afterword

John Lewis

148

List of Plates

157

Selected Bibliography

Director's Foreword

This book and the exhibition it accompanies provide the occasion for the most important art museum presentation in more than twenty-five years of the photographs of the civil rights movement. The last exhibition of this kind held in a major American museum was titled *We'll Never Turn Back*, at the National Museum of History and Technology (now the National Museum of American History) at the Smithsonian Institution in 1980. Today, forty years after the assassination of Dr. Martin Luther King Jr., memories remain fresh of the seismic shift in our social landscape that Dr. King and his colleagues brought into being. This exhibition takes a fresh and innovative look at the photography and media culture of this seminal era in our nation's history.

Road to Freedom: Photographs of the Civil Rights Movement, 1956–1968 was conceived and organized by Julian Cox, the High Museum of Art's curator of photography, who skillfully gathered and selected materials from a variety of sources. Through the planning and execution phases of the exhibition and publication, deputy director Kinshasha Holman Conwill and chief curator Jacquelyn Serwer of the National Museum of African American History and Culture provided important intellectual and logistical support, for which we are very grateful.

Many of the photographs in the exhibition, which represent the work of more than thirty photographers, have never been on public view. They were taken by black and white photographers, some well known and some obscure. The images share a passion for justice and a strong moral tone—they are among the most important and memorable photographs of the era. In this exhibition, archival documents complement the photographs and reveal much about the culture and media of the period. These potent objects vividly show a nation pitted against itself, grappling with change.

The majority of the photographs in the exhibition come from the High's collection, which has expanded greatly in this area in recent years, and which now has one of the finest civil rights photography holdings of any American art museum. However, the potential of the exhibition could not have been realized without several lenders who generously shared important photographs from their collections. We sincerely thank the Birmingham Civil Rights Institute, the Schomburg Center for Research in Black Culture at the New York Public Library, the St. Louis Art Museum, and the Getty Research Institute. The following individuals also kindly agreed to part with prized possessions for the duration of the exhibition: Sir Elton John, Charles Cowles, Howard Greenberg, Vicki Hunt, James Otis, Dan and Mary Solomon, and Dr. Charles and Lucille Plotz. We are especially grateful to photographers Bob Adelman, Dan Budnik, Bruce Davidson, LeRoy Henderson, and Danny Lyon for lending work from their personal collections. Papers and archival documents were loaned from the Atlanta History Center, Emory University, and the National Archives, Southeast Division. We also gratefully acknowledge the unprecedented access that Johnson Publications has provided to reproduce the photographs of Moneta Sleet, Jr., and the cover of *Jet* magazine.

We hope this exhibition and publication will do much to refocus our thoughts and memories on the brave actions, great and small, that defined the movement. These photographs capture the hope and courage of the men and women who challenged the status quo, armed only with the philosophy of nonviolence and the strength of their convictions. The photographs were made by committed artists, activists, and journalists, who risked injury and even death to document this important moment of growth in our nation. It is the vision and tenacity of these dedicated and gifted people—on both sides of the camera—that live today in this exhibition.

Michael E. Shapiro
Nancy and Holcombe T. Green, Jr. Director
High Museum of Art

Preface and Acknowledgments

This exhibition and publication arose out of a desire to appropriately mark the fortieth anniversary of the assassination of Dr. Martin Luther King Jr., an Atlanta native and a leading figure in the civil rights movement. That simple idea evolved into a quest to evaluate the photography and media culture of the movement, and to investigate the different strategies adopted by photographers who documented this tumultuous era in American history. This process involved an extensive search for photographs that could be acquired by the High Museum, building on the pioneering efforts in this direction made by Ellen Fleurov, the High's first curator of photography, who acquired several important works for the permanent collection in the 1990s. In recent years, however, our holdings in this area have grown from a modest 25 to 30 images to a substantial archive of more than 250 photographs.

The following individuals have my sincere thanks for providing the financial support necessary to reach our goals for the growth of the collection in civil rights photographs: Charles and Kristie Abney, Sandra Anderson Baccus, Lucinda Bunnen, Debbie and Jeff Chapman, Jess and Sherri Crawford, Earnest and Charlene Crusoe-Ingram, Charlotte and Jim Dixon, Wanda Hopkins, Jane Kerr, Dr. Elaine Levin, Jeff and Valerie Levy, Joe Massey, Jonathan Shils, Dr. Henrie M. Treadwell, and Joan N. Whitcomb.

The process of expanding the High's collection in this material has not come without challenges. For example, black photographers—whether freelancing or employed by black-owned newspapers and magazines—photographed the civil rights movement, but much of the work has not been preserved as vintage prints and remains relatively inaccessible to this day. Moreover, because these pioneering photographers had limited access to the people and places where white photographers flourished, their work did not always reach the same wide circulation as the productions of their mainstream coun-terparts. But their images were important in galvanizing the black community to action. Further scholarship is required to recognize the contributions of black photographers and the black press.

Working on this project provided an opportunity to learn from a host of individ-uals who were active either in front of or behind the camera. Many photographers contributed to my understanding of this material by generously sharing their knowledge of the period as well as information about the events and individuals portrayed. I am very grateful to Bob Adelman, Donald Blumberg, Charles Brittin, Dan Budnik, Bruce Davidson, Doris Derby, Bill Eppridge, Ben Fernandez, Larry Fink, Bob Fitch, LeRoy Henderson, Matt Herron, Bob Johnson, Charlie Kelly, Julius Lester, Builder Levy, Danny Lyon, Constantine Manos, Charles Moore, Paul Robertson, Sam Parrish, Steve Schapiro, and Tamio Wakayama. Numerous civil rights veterans—journalists and reporters as well as activists—graciously hosted my visits, entertained my questions, and willingly shared their memories and insights. I am deeply indebted to Archie Allen, D'Army Bailey, Charles Black, Margaret Block, James Bond, Julian Bond, Catherine Burks Brooks, Dorothy Cotton, John Gibson, Kathryn Johnson, Pauline Knight, Annie Ragans Laster, John Lewis, Sam Mahone, Sandra Russell Mansfield, Bob Mants, Elizabeth Martinez, Steve McNichols, Joe Morse, Diane Nash, Moses Newson, George Roberts, Carol Seay, George Smith, John Steele, Hank Thomas, Jimmie Travis, Rev. C. T. Vivian, Hollis Watkins, Ed Whitfield, and Ambassador Andrew Young.

At the High Museum of Art I would like to thank Michael Shapiro, Director, Philip Verre, Chief Operating Officer, and David Brenneman, Chief Curator and Director of Collections and Exhibitions, for their spirited support and sound collegial advice. Danielle Avram, Curatorial Assistant of Photography (and her predecessor, Beth Hancock) provided with great aplomb research and administrative support for all facets of the exhibition and publication. Jill Paschal, a summer intern from Spelman College, conducted valuable research in local archives and drafted texts for the exhibition. Marjorie Harvey and Laurie Kind coordinated the exhibition, while its elegant design and presentation is the work of Jim Waters and Angela Jaeger. This volume was realized under the direction of Kelly Morris, Manager of Publications, who saw it through from start to finish with enthusiasm and infinite patience. Heather Medlock and Rachel Bohan brought their skill and experience to the task of editing the manuscript. I am deeply grateful to them all.

I would like to thank Ed Marquand and the staff of Marquand Books for undertaking this venture. I am greatly indebted to Jeff Wincapaw, who designed the catalogue with a sure hand and a keen eye, and steered the process of translating the photographs to the printed page. Peter Harholdt, ably assisted by Donna Tribby, carried out the photo-documentation and went to great lengths to produce the highest standards of reproduction. I also want to thank Dr. Charles Johnson for the well-chosen words in his Introduction, contributed in a spirit of goodwill and with a specificity that is so well matched to the photographs. Congressman John Lewis, who has supported this project in a number of meaningful ways, has my sincere gratitude for his thoughts and reflections in the Afterword.

Several colleagues at other institutions have provided information and support essential to the realization of the exhibition and publication, including Steve Ennis, Randall Burkett, and Teresa Burk at the Manuscript, Archives and Rare Book Library, Emory University; Mary Yearwood at the Schomburg Center for Research in Black Culture at the New York Public Library; Michael Rose and Billie Gaines at the Atlanta History Center; Richard Rayburn, Jim McCandless, and Mary Evelyn Tomlin at the National Archives, Southeast Division; Eric Lutz and Pat Woods at the St. Louis Art Museum; Sarah Meister and Jennifer Tobias at the Museum of Modern Art, New York; Irene Lotspeich-Phillips at the Getty Research Institute; Lawrence Pijeaux, Ahmad Ward, and Laura Caldwell Anderson at the Birmingham Civil Rights Institute; Marina Pacini at the Memphis Brooks Museum of Art; Francine Henderson and Kellie Totten-Williams at the Auburn Avenue Research Library; Peter Higdon at Ryerson University; Ruta Abolins at the University of Georgia; Jim Mones at the *New York Times*; Jim Auchmutey and Robert Cauvel at the *Atlanta Journal-Constitution*; and John Brewer at the *Pittsburgh Courier*.

For their valuable comments on my essay in this book, I want to thank Kinshasha Holman Conwill, Brett Gadsden, Barret Oliver, Michael Lomax, and Alexis Scott. Their enthusiasm and perceptive comments were indispensable. Any errors of fact or oddities of perspective are mine alone.

I am also happy to thank the following friends and colleagues for sharing valuable information and relevant ideas during the preparation of this project: Brett Abbott, Matt Arnett, Raymond Arsenault, Adrienne Aurichio, Stephen Berkman, Bill Boling, Gail Buckland, Elna Broffman, Fred Burger, Katie Chapman, Paul Conlan, Tony Decaneas, Rita Dove, Erina Duganne, Ellen Fleurov, Bill Gillespie, Bobby Glustrom, Michael Hargraves, Gregory Hite, Jonathan Hollada, Vicki Hunt, Jane Jackson, Robert Flynn Johnson, Tom Johnson, Jane Kerr, George King, Hank Klibanoff, Lisa Kurzner, Nancy Leiberman, Peter MacGill, Herman "Skip" Mason, Kristine McKenna, Susan Ross, Doug Shipman, Chip Simone, Edward Spriggs, Gerald Straw, Stephen White, Cecil Williams, and Reggie Williams.

A number of collectors kindly granted me access to their holdings and took time to share their thoughts as well as their treasures: Charles Cowles, Sir Elton John, James Otis, Dr. Charles and Lucille Plotz, Dan and Mary Solomon, and Jerry Whiting. The dealers and estate executors who openly shared important material with me include Joseph Bellows, Edwynn Houk, Keith De Lellis, Monica Karales, Craig Krull, Tracy Martin, Jo Tartt, and David Winter. Special thanks go to Howard Greenberg and particularly Steve Kasher, whose passion for the subject and instinct for preserving this history are unmatched.

On a more personal note I would like to thank those who provided invaluable support and served as crucial sounding boards throughout this project, in particular Michael Lomax and Joe Massey. Neal Broffman accompanied me on numerous trips to interview veteran activists and some of the photographers, and he produced the wonderful short film that accompanies the exhibition. Most of all I thank my family—Daphne, Maya, and Fiona—for their patience, love, and unconditional support, which daily sustain me.

It is my hope that this study sheds at least a sliver of new light on this important subject, and invites a deeper appreciation of the talents and commitment of the men and women—on both sides of the camera—who dedicated a large part of their lives to bringing about this vital sea change in our society.

Julian Cox
Curator of Photography
High Museum of Art

Charles Johnson

Introduction

Whenever we look at photographs of the civil rights movement, it is important to understand these powerful images in terms of this nation's unique experiment in democracy. Half a century has passed since this nonviolent revolution transformed America, and viewers born after the 1960s might feel they are seeing images that record not just a different time but an entirely different world.

In order to properly appreciate these photographs, we must place them within the context of a 388-year struggle for justice and equality that began in 1619, the year twenty Africans were sold from a Dutch ship to colonists in the Jamestown colony. Those early arrivals from Africa became indentured servants—men like Emanuel Driggus, Anthony Johnson, and Francis Payne, who eventually purchased freedom for themselves and their families, amassed property, and established plantations. But soon enough those stolen from Africa during the Atlantic slave trade (the conservative estimate is 20 million people, but some scholars place the number as high as 100 million) found their condition of chattel bondage to be permanent and based on their race.

Although the Founding Fathers frequently described the evils of slavery when denouncing the treatment they had received from King George III, they were not prepared to abolish the profitable "peculiar institution" in their own colonies. Yet, as revolutionaries dedicated to Lockean liberalism and Enlightenment principles, they were able to transcend these contradictions and prejudices when they drafted the sacred texts of our civil religion—the Declaration of Independence and Bill of Rights—with "self-evident" truths that "all men are created equal, that they are endowed by their Creator with certain inalienable Rights, that among these are Life, Liberty, and the pursuit of Happiness." These inspiring, lofty ideals fueled the passion for freedom equally in blacks and whites.

That first revolution of 1776, and the cloudy, equivocal language of just four clauses in the Constitution (Articles I and IV), failed to extend freedom to black people and kept in place "the great sin and shame of slavery," as Frederick Douglass called it. And so the fledgling American republic was plunged into civil war, a cataclysm that cost 620,000 lives, in an effort to correct the unfinished business of the Revolution.

Unfortunately, the Civil War, while freeing the slaves, did not close the gap between the nation's democratic ideals and its practices. Many whites, Harriet Beecher Stowe and Abraham Lincoln among them, abhorred the obvious horrors of slavery but saw blacks as inferior and felt they should be repatriated to the American colony of Liberia and that America should remain a white man's country. Furthermore, the newly freed slaves, propertyless and uneducated, were given scant assistance after their emancipation. "It was never intended that they [ex-slaves] should thenceforth be fed, clothed, educated and sheltered by the United States," argued President Andrew Johnson when he vetoed Senate Bill 60, which would have given land to the freedmen. "The idea on which the slaves were assisted to freedom was that, on becoming free, they would be a self-sustaining population. Any legislation that shall imply that they are not expected to attain a self-sustaining condition must have a tendency injurious alike to their character and prospects."

In other words, the former slaves were on their own. As the old black saying put it, they were expected to "make a way out of no way." This would prove to be a difficult way indeed. For the next sixty years, between 1895—when Booker T. Washington delivered his famous proclamation that blacks and whites could "be separate but equal like the fingers on the hand" (which appeased the South)—and the Montgomery bus boycott of 1955, black Americans fell victim to a fragile, false, and ultimately doomed social and political arrangement: racial segregation, the American equivalent of South African apartheid.

In this publication and in the accompanying exhibition, pay close attention to the images of economic deprivation and systematic oppression—the run-down shacks blacks lived in, the "Colored" and "White" signs over drinking fountains preposterously different in size (fig. 1), and the disturbing presence of the Ku Klux Klan, whether marching openly in city streets or burning crosses in the dead of night. Clearly, separate did *not* mean equal. Worse, during the era of segregation, black Americans were systematically disenfranchised, denied gainful employment, refused access to the best education, denigrated in social situations, and relegated in every facet of civic life to second-class citizenship. A system as unjust and irrational as segregation, one that daily demonized and de-humanized black Americans, could only be sustained by social violence as great as that used during slavery. The world it created was Kafkaesque, and just as damaging to whites as it was to blacks, for whites were forced from childhood to believe in their innate superiority and to feel entitled by race to unearned privileges.

Yet another revolution, then, was required to address the unfinished business of the Civil War and Reconstruction. It began on December 1, 1955, when a 42-year-old seamstress and secretary of her local branch of the National Association for the Advancement of Colored People (NAACP) named Rosa Parks refused to give up her seat to a white man in the black section of a crowded bus. Her non-cooperation with evil,

Fig. 1. Danny Lyon (American, born 1942), *Drinking Fountains, Dougherty County Courthouse, Albany, Georgia*, 1962, gelatin silver print, 14 × 11 inches (35.6 × 27.9 cm), High Museum of Art, Atlanta, gift of Turner Broadcasting System, Inc., 2006.238.4.

as Thoreau would have called it, electrified and unified the 50,000 black men and women in Montgomery around an epic 382-day bus boycott spearheaded by the Montgomery Improvement Association (MIA), which elected to its presidency a 25-year-old minister named Martin Luther King Jr. He was a newly minted Ph.D. in theology from Boston University and the son of Martin Luther King Sr.—"Daddy King," one of the most prominent activist-ministers in Atlanta. Serving at the helm of first the MIA and then the Southern Christian Leadership Conference (SCLC), King and his lieutenants staged dramatic campaigns for desegregation and equality across the South for a decade, leaving his spiritual and moral vision indelibly imprinted on this third revolution to realize the nation's most cherished principles.

Addressing five thousand people at the Holt Baptist Church during the Montgomery boycott, King thundered, "If you will protest courageously, and yet with dignity and Christian love, future historians will say, 'There lived a great people—a black people— who injected new meaning and dignity into the veins of civilization.'" Often he said, "Christ gave us the goals and Mahatma Gandhi the tactics." With his emphasis on nonviolence, on *agape* (unconditional love), and his belief in the "beloved community" as the ultimate goal Americans must strive for, young King guaranteed that black Americans would have the moral high ground when facing segregationists and white supremacists who had greater power and wealth. The movement's leaders were far better prepared than their opponents. They had studied Gandhi's tactics against the British in India. They knew history and the law. And they were aware that violence and bloodshed had characterized black revolts against oppression since the seventeenth century. Outnumbered ten to one, black Americans could never achieve freedom through armed struggle. But a nonviolent approach, with its grounding in the ideal of Christian brotherhood and the Declaration of Independence, gave this fresh phase of the black freedom struggle the character of a distinctly American revolution that all people of good will, black and white, had to acknowledge as the moral vision they preferred for themselves and their country, particularly during the Cold War, when the Soviets repeatedly criticized America for its treatment of black people.

These photographs show people of good will, inspired by the Montgomery boycott and the Supreme Court's ruling in 1956 that segregation on buses was unconstitutional (and earlier by the Court's decision in *Brown v. Board of Education of Topeka* that school segregation violated the Constitution), who responded en masse to the most transformative domestic development in America in the twentieth century, often placing their own lives at risk. We know the leaders—King, Ralph Abernathy, Bayard Rustin, Fred Shuttlesworth, C.T. Vivian, and others—but these individuals were supported by countless anonymous volunteers, especially by black women, who constituted the majority of the membership in churches, where so much of the organizing took place. In the truest sense of the word, they were patriots, men and women imagining the truly unimaginable in human history: a world without racial discrimination or the dominance of one group by another. Naturally, this idealism inspired the young. Students volunteered, risking their lives to integrate lunch counters and interstate buses, and founded their own organization, the Student Nonviolent Coordinating Committee (SNCC). At the forefront of the movement, they attended workshops to prepare themselves for nonviolent civil disobedience (fig. 2) and fanned out across the South's most dangerous segregated counties

Fig. 2. James Karales (American, 1930–2002), *Passive Resistance Training, Student Nonviolent Coordinating Committee (SNCC)*, 1960, gelatin silver print, 10 × 13⅝ inches (25.3 × 34.7 cm), High Museum of Art, Atlanta, purchase with funds from Jess and Sherri Crawford in honor of John Lewis, 2007.245.

Fig. 3. Unknown photographer, *Parents of Denise McNair, Victim of Bombing of the 16th Street Baptist Church, Birmingham, Alabama*, September 16, 1963, gelatin silver print, 10 × 8 inches (25.4 × 20.3 cm), High Museum of Art, Atlanta, purchase with funds from Jonathan Shils in memory of Taylor Stuckey, 2007.237.

to register black voters, bringing them the precious franchise promised to every citizen in the Fifteenth Amendment.

During one Freedom Summer, three young civil rights workers—Michael Schwerner, James Chaney, and Andrew Goodman—were murdered in Mississippi. Four black girls—Addie Mae Collins, Carol Robertson, Cynthia Wesley, and Denise McNair—were killed in the bombing of the Sixteenth Street Baptist Church Sunday School in Birmingham on September 15, 1963 (fig. 3). Although they were practitioners of nonviolence, civil rights workers and their families were dogged by violence and death. During the tempestuous 1960s, violence and death spread into the political arena, which saw the assassinations of President John F. Kennedy, his brother Robert, the former Nation of Islam leader Malcolm X, King, the Black Panther spokesman Fred Hampton in Chicago, and the murders of far too many others. So relentless was the violence of this period, the "long hot summers" of cities burning, that the federal government prepared itself for the possibility of civil war.

Fortunately, at this pivotal moment in the nation's history, Americans chose social evolution over racial chaos. They enshrined that decision in the Civil Rights Act of 1964 and the Voting Rights Act of 1965, two monumental acts of legislation that finally made good on the Founders' "promissory note" that King spoke of so eloquently in his 1963 "I Have a Dream" speech, delivered during the March on Washington—a note of liberty "to which every American was to fall heir."

The civil rights movement is now forty years behind us, but its legacy permeates every fiber of American society. Its impact has rippled far beyond these shores, inspiring freedom fighters in South Africa and those who took to the streets in Czechoslovakia during that country's "Velvet Revolution." The movement's language and strategies were eagerly adopted by women, farm workers, gay Americans, and the elderly and disabled in their struggles for equality, respect, and justice. Like the Revolution and the Civil War, the civil rights movement revitalized and refined the dream of democracy. More than anything else, this watershed moment in history reminds us that we ourselves must shepherd and nurture that dream at the dawn of the twenty-first century.

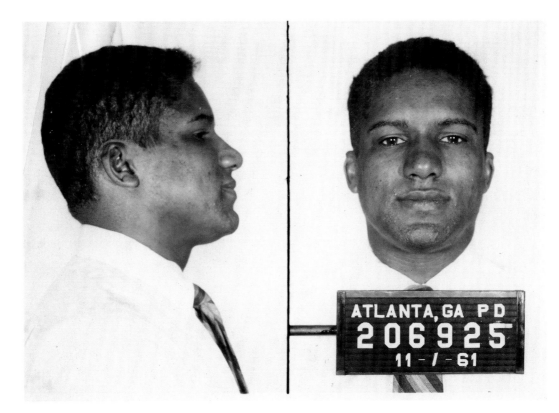

James Forman

John Lewis

Julian Cox

Bearing Witness:
Photography and the Civil Rights Movement

What happens to a dream deferred?

Does it dry up
like a raisin in the sun?
Or fester like a sore—
And then run?
Does it stink like rotten meat
Or crust and sugar over—
like a syrupy sweet?

Maybe it just sags
Like a heavy load.

Or does it explode?

—Langston Hughes[1]

The civil rights movement and direct action social protest took many forms in the 1950s and 1960s: protest marches, nose-to-nose showdowns between demonstrators who offered no resistance and city police, national guardsmen, state troopers, and sheriff's deputies wielding billy clubs, cattle prods, tear gas, fire hoses, and dogs in response. It also involved court fights against segregation in schools and libraries and on buses and trains, and opposition to segregation at drinking fountains, in restrooms, and in voting booths. It sparked sit-ins at lunch counters, boycotts, and "freedom rides" on buses traveling from the North to the South. Asserting civil rights became a cause, a social revolution unlike anything the country had experienced since the Civil War. It involved thousands of acts of individual courage undertaken in the pursuit of freedom. While nonviolent protest was the dominant tactic, shock waves of violence broke out across the nation, with civil disturbances erupting in Detroit, Chicago, Newark, and Los Angeles. For the media and for photographers, it was an engaging, demanding, and sometimes highly dangerous story.

Fig.1. Lonnie J. Wilson (American, 1924–2005), *Molotov Cocktails*, 1967, gelatin silver print, $2^{15}/_{16} \times 4^{1}/_{2}$ inches (7.5 × 11.4 cm), private collection.

Consequential images of the civil rights movement were made by an array of photographers—artists, photojournalists, movement photographers, and amateurs—each with a distinct point of view. While their individual approaches may have differed, they all seem to have shared an awareness of the historical significance of the moment, and understood that they were documenting a nation in tumult and transition. As Steven Kasher has put it, "The great photographs of the movement were crafted with urgent passion—for their own time and for the future."[2] Typically, the photographs they produced are valued as historical evidence and for their capacity to effect cultural and political change. That is, their function as social documents is commonly emphasized above their status as critical or aesthetic representations. But occasionally, and profoundly, they show us something that we have not seen before—a point of view that prompts us to look at the world, and the subject, with renewed concentration. The images present the full range of poverty, brutality, and outright hatred, but also glimpses of hope, unity, and a collective determination to stand up and move forward in the face of seemingly impenetrable obstacles.

Photojournalists were trained to record newsworthy events according to the "professional principle of objectivity,"[3] even if that meant putting themselves in danger in order to get the picture. Black photographers—and reporters—often worked under volatile and perilous conditions (see pl. 6). Moses Newson, who covered the civil rights beat for the *Tri-State Defender* in Memphis and later for the *Baltimore Afro-American*, was brutally attacked while reporting on the desegregation of Central High School in Little Rock, Arkansas, in 1957, and again during the Freedom Rides in 1961.[4] Charles Moore, who was a staff photographer for the *Montgomery Advertiser* in the early 1960s (and who also supplied images to publications such as *Life* magazine), remembers that it was the simple realization of knowing and believing in the difference between right and wrong that compelled him to make his work. Feelings of fear and vulnerability hardly entered his mind—he was too committed to telling the story to allow concern for his personal safety to interfere with his mission.[5]

More than any other medium, photography promises an unhindered immediacy of representation. It readily obeys the rules of nonfiction. Its job is to make the world visible, which it does more democratically than all other visual arts. Sometimes the most artless, undemonstrative pictures can reveal the most about a subject. A photograph of six half-empty beer bottles, stuffed at the neck with rags, neatly arranged in a row on a table (fig. 1) raises questions: Who made this and why? For whom was it produced? How does it relate to the ostensible subject under discussion—civil rights photography? This snapshot is stamped and dated on the verso "Lonnie J. Wilson/1967," and was made by a lifetime detective who worked for the Birmingham, Alabama, police department.[6] It is a piece of evidence, a testimony, and an exemplar of photography as a stop-time device—qualities that make every photograph, whether sophisticated or humdrum, unique. Police mug shots (see p. 18) share similar qualities. Great snapshots such as these may be among the highest forms of photography because they are so ripe with suggestion. We know that they come with a story. They tell us something significant about the human condition. Their wonder is that they conjure in plain, pithy visual language the same kind of imaginative voyaging that is active in the eloquent verse of Langston Hughes.

Pictures for the Press

The brutal murder of fourteen-year-old Emmett Till in Money, Mississippi, in the summer of 1955, brought reporters to the South in unprecedented numbers. It was also the first time the white-led northern press had responded significantly to a racial story, and the first time they worked alongside their black counterparts and shared the same degree of access and opportunity.[7] Till's murder was reported extensively in the black press. Working competitively on stories were reporters from *Jet*, *Ebony*, the *Chicago Defender*, *The Pittsburgh Courier*, *Amsterdam News*, and the *Afro-American* newspapers. A freelance photographer from Memphis, Ernest C. Withers, covered the trial extensively for his hometown newspaper, the *Tri-State Defender* (working alongside reporter Moses Newson), and made important pictures in the courtroom during the trial in Sumner, Mississippi. His colleague, David Jackson, a staffer for *Jet* and *Ebony* magazines, made the harrowing close-up portrait of Till's mutilated face when his open casket was put on view in Chicago. The photograph was published in *Jet* and sold out the magazine instantly, but few whites saw the image because its circulation was carefully controlled by Johnson Publications.[8] The publication of Till's photograph in *Jet* began a tradition in this magazine of reporting in depth on prominent civil rights stories, a commitment that continued unabated through the late 1960s (fig. 2).

The Till murder had an extraordinary impact on a new generation of young blacks, adolescents at the time, who would soon call for justice and freedom in ways hitherto unknown in America. Less than three months later the black community of Montgomery began a groundbreaking boycott of the municipal bus system. It was there in the dark of early morning in December 1956, that Withers boarded a bus alongside reporter L. Alex Wilson to capture Dr. King and Rev. Abernathy's historic ride on the first desegregated

Fig. 2. *Jet*, March 25, 1965, front cover.

bus to operate after the boycott (pl. 3). This set a pattern for Withers, who was on hand when it counted to make important photographs of the civil rights struggle for more than a decade, concluding with his documentation of the Memphis sanitation workers' strike in the spring of 1968 (pl. 93).[9]

By the end of World War II, photographs occupied roughly one-third of news space in the average metropolitan newspaper in the United States. Editors understood the photograph's ability to convey explicit information about a personality or event, as well as its capacity to dramatically increase sales. The growth of independent news agencies such as United Press International (UPI) and the Associated Press (AP) was swift, bringing about a significant shift in the way that photographs were shared and disseminated. In 1935 the Associated Press Wirephoto network was launched, which allowed for the express transmission of news images over telephone lines.[10] Photographs could be exchanged and published with greater speed and ease than ever before.

Wirephoto technology was in its heyday during the civil rights era, and the growing popularity of television helped accelerate the progress of a movement whose time had come. By 1960 roughly 80 percent of American households had television, and low incomes in the South were no obstacle to blacks, who increasingly used television as a means to see news that reflected their reality in a way that the white or mainstream newspapers did not.[11] Despite the growth in numbers of viewers, television had not yet superseded the printed page nationwide as the medium through which most Americans got their news.[12] Magazines such as *Look*, *Life*, *Jet*, and *Ebony* did brisk business and revolutionized the use of photography by publishing dramatic stories that were built around a clutch of carefully edited images.

Agencies such as AP and UPI were under intense pressure to deliver newsworthy photographs for the daily newspapers across the nation. In the South, AP had major bureaus in Atlanta, Memphis, and Miami, staffed with reporters, photographers, and photo editors. The personnel were typically white men, who spent much of their time working independently on assignment.[13] When they were sent to small towns or remote rural locations—as was often the case during the civil rights movement—the photographers carried mobile darkroom equipment, allowing them to process the film and make wet prints on location, often in a makeshift studio darkroom set up in a motel.[14] Once developed and processed, the still-moist print was wrapped onto a drum scanner

Fig. 3. James "Spider" Martin (American, 1939–2003), *Reporter Al Fox Calling in a Story, Selma to Montgomery March*, 1965, gelatin silver print, 10 × 8 inches (25.4 × 20.3 cm), Spider Martin Civil Rights Collection.

Fig. 4. Morton Broffman (American, 1928–1992), *Photographer at Work, Selma to Montgomery March, Alabama*, 1965, gelatin silver print, 9 9/16 × 7 3/8 inches (24.3 × 18.8 cm), High Museum of Art, 2007.63. Gift of the Broffman family.

and transmitted by telephone to the nearest bureau. The goal was to get the image—and the story—to New York as soon as possible, where it could be printed and evaluated by editors for publication. For reporters too, being on hand to get the news and send it from the scene and onto the wire was essential to staying ahead of rivals in the field. On the Selma to Montgomery March for Voting Rights in March 1965, the more intrepid reporters adapted to the remoteness of Highway 80 in rural Alabama and rigged up a working telephone by tapping directly into the phone lines along the route (fig. 3).[15] Their stories could be filed on the spot, saving precious travel time to and from a regional bureau.

Associated Press photographers routinely wrote their own captions for the photographs, and this information became an integral element in the evaluation of the image for publication by newsroom editors. Although many news photographers had been trained to use a Graflex Speed Graphic—a 4-×-5-inch format camera that was commonplace equipment for news photographers from around 1930 onward—by 1960 they increasingly worked with 35mm cameras. This reduction in the size of their equipment improved mobility and allowed them to be less obtrusive while in the field.[16] It was common for photographers to carry as many as two or three cameras, each fitted with slightly different lenses to be deployed as circumstances demanded (fig. 4). Establishing and then maintaining contact with movement leaders was a key to landing a good story, as was knowing how and when to disappear when danger loomed. Kathryn Johnson, an Associated Press reporter based in Atlanta, recalled a lucky escape in Montgomery, Alabama, while

Fig. 5. Horace Cort (American, active 1940s–1970s), *Lester Maddox Escorts Albert Dunn from the Parking Lot of His Pickrick Restaurant, Atlanta*, July 3, 1964, gelatin silver print, 9⅛ × 11⅜ inches (23.2 × 28.9 cm), High Museum of Art, purchase with funds from Sandra Anderson Baccus in loving memory of Lloyd T. Baccus, M.D., 2007.99.

trying to file a story on the Freedom Rides in May 1961: "I was phoning the Atlanta AP office from an outside phone booth when several angry white men spotted me dictating. They ran over, grabbed the phone booth, yanked it off its moorings, and rattled it vigorously with me inside. I was rescued by AP photographer Horace Cort, who drove close by, threw open his car door, and yelled, 'Katy! Get in.'"[17]

Horace Cort, whose intercession proved timely for his colleague, was a veteran photojournalist based out of Atlanta's AP bureau who had a knack for getting the picture that told the story. He supplied his editors with images that spoke in a familiar visual language while resonating with the public on both cultural and emotional levels. On July 3, 1964, he photographed the outcome when three young black students from the Interdenominational Theological Center in Atlanta—Albert Dunn, George Willis, and Woodrow Lewis—tried to enter the Pickrick Restaurant, owned and operated by the notorious segregationist Lester Maddox, on Hemphill Avenue in downtown Atlanta. They were there to test the muscle of the Civil Rights Act, which President Johnson had

Fig. 6. Verso of fig. 5.

signed into law the day before, on July 2. Lester Maddox barred their entry and insisted that they would not be welcome anytime. The young men informed him that they would return at 5:30 that afternoon. Maddox was there to meet them, along with a crowd of approximately 200 axe-wielding supporters. He promptly escorted them from his premises at gunpoint.[18] Horace Cort tracked the action carefully, and waited for the optimal moment to produce a picture that would effectively represent the story (fig. 5). His photograph shows Maddox, pistol in hand, with his son, Lester Jr., brandishing an axe handle, escorting Albert Dunn across the parking lot and off his property. The picture is tactical and deliberate and has a staged quality, with the presence, at right, of the outstretched, truncated limbs of three reporters, one wielding a notebook and pen and the others microphones. Part showman and part thug, Maddox was a master manipulator of the media and frequently choreographed such stunts in order to promote himself and his business. To those familiar with Maddox and his antics (he was nick-named "the Cracker Don Quixote"), this episode—deeply disturbing though it was—was not surprising.

Cort's photograph was reproduced the following day in the *New York Times* and subsequently on several occasions when updates on the story ran in that newspaper and in the *Atlanta Journal*.[19] As with many press photographs, the verso of this print is marked with the caption, ink stamps, inscriptions, and editorial notations that show how and when it was used. These markings give the picture the well-worn quality of a frequently handled object (fig. 6). The blurred forms, harsh contrasts, and grainy quality of many press photographs also directly reveal the conditions under which they were made. They increase the credibility of the photographs as documents—as unmediated records of a visceral experience. Notwithstanding their subjective underpinnings, news photographs are widely perceived as objective—because they allow viewers to see, verify, and interpret occurrences with their own eyes.

Despite Maddox's aggressive and illogical actions, he was able to report that business was brisk—up 40 percent—as a result of his gun-toting antics. He had significant support from Atlanta's white community and was acquitted on two counts of "pointing a pistol at another" in Fulton County Court.[20] He also had friends in neighboring Alabama who fell right in line behind his cause. At a rally at Lakewood Park, a white working-class neighborhood in Atlanta, Governor George Wallace lauded Maddox's actions and denounced the Civil Rights Act as a sham and a hoax.[21] Maddox, however, was fighting a losing battle. The three men who tried to enter his restaurant on July 3 filed suit against him, and on July 7, 1964, he was bound over to the Fulton County Criminal Court. The NAACP took up the suit two days later. While Maddox remained openly defiant and calculated in his resistance to the Civil Rights Act, his approach lacked sophistication and was legally flawed.[22] Rather than adhere to federal law and desegregate, Maddox ultimately sold his restaurant in February 1965, saying: "I have given up my business rather than obey the Federal government orders to serve Negroes. To have done any less would have made me less than an American."[23] He believed in his right to serve whomever he pleased, and that did not include blacks.

Early in the spring of 1961 the Supreme Court in the case of *Boynton v. Commonwealth of Virginia* held that discrimination against interstate travelers in bus terminal restaurants was illegal. To gauge the effects of this ruling the Congress of Racial Equality (CORE) mobilized interracial groups of passengers to test the compliance of the southern states with the new federal interstate transportation laws.[24] On May 14, 1961, a quiet Mother's Day throughout most of Alabama, an episode of extreme violence catapulted the Freedom Rides into the national consciousness. A Greyhound bus traveling from Atlanta to Birmingham, carrying fourteen passengers (including reporter Moses Newson, covering the Freedom Rides for the *Baltimore Afro-American*), pulled in to the terminal at Anniston, Alabama, where the station doors had been locked shut. The bus was immediately set upon by a mob led by a local Klansman named William Chappell, its tires slashed and windows smashed. There were no police in sight. When law enforcement finally arrived (after approximately twenty minutes), they gave the bus a cursory inspection for damage and ordered the driver, O. T. Jones of Birmingham, to leave the terminal, escorting him to the town limits, where the vehicle was left to the mercy of the following mob. The bus limped along the highway for about six miles before being forced off the road on the outskirts of Bynum by a convoy of cars and trucks that had grown to forty or fifty in number. The bus was stormed by the mob, the passengers were trapped inside, and the bus was firebombed. It was a scene of carnage.[25]

Tracking the entire episode was Joe Postiglione, a freelance photographer who worked for the commercial photography chain Hollywood Studio and contributed his pictures to the local newspaper, the *Anniston Star*.[26] Postiglione more than likely was tipped off about the planned attack, because he was at the Anniston terminal when the bus arrived and he followed it out onto the highway with the mob. He captured the drama in a shocking series of pictures that until recently was known only through a handful of photographs that he made available to the news services.[27] Two pictures were sold to AP and UPI (fig. 7), and seven were reproduced the following day in the

Anniston Star.[28] The photographs were cropped quite radically by the news services, but at least three of them ran closer to full frame in the local newspaper. Postiglione appears to have made the pictures with a 2¼-inch medium format camera. His credit line under the photographs reads "Little Joe"—which is how he preferred to be known, both on account of his diminutive size (he was barely five feet tall) and because he surmised that readers in Alabama would have trouble pronouncing his last name.[29] Amazingly, none of the passengers was killed, but all fourteen suffered from smoke inhalation, and several were beaten when they finally exited the bus. A local girl, twelve-year-old Janie Miller, provided the choking victims with water in the face of taunts and abuse from Klansmen. Subsequently threatened and ostracized for this act of kindness, she and her family were forced to leave their community in the aftermath of the bombing.[30] The riders' nightmare did not end there. Medics at the local hospital, Anniston Memorial, refused to admit the black passengers, submitting to pressure from the Klan, who threatened to burn down the building. They were eventually rescued in the dead of night by a squadron of cars sent by Rev. Fred Shuttlesworth, pastor of the Sixteenth Street Baptist Church in Birmingham, who was informed of the danger they were in and knew well the perils of racism in Alabama's black belt. They were whisked away to the relative safety of Birmingham, lucky to be alive.

Fig. 7. Joseph Postiglione (American, born Italy, 1922–1995), *Passengers outside a Burning Greyhound Bus, Anniston, Alabama*, May 14, 1961, gelatin silver print, 5⁷⁄₁₆ × 8½ inches (13.9 × 21.6 cm), High Museum of Art, purchase with funds from Sandra Anderson Baccus in loving memory of Lloyd T. Baccus, M.D., 2007.95.

The Student Movement

Get out the lunch-box of your dreams.
Bite into the sandwich of your heart,
And ride the Jim Crow car until it screams
Then—like an atom bomb—it bursts apart.

—Langston Hughes[31]

In its earliest days, the sit-in movement was a spontaneous student-led enterprise that quickly became a particularly effective form of nonviolent direct action. As an indication of a new and burgeoning activism on the part of young blacks, it was a strong example of their genuine willingness to turn to unfamiliar and untried ways to express their grievances and to seek redress. While this form of peaceful protest began in Greensboro, North Carolina, in the winter of 1960, within six months cities throughout the South were participating. Nashville became a particularly prominent center, led by a triumvirate of ministers—C. T. Vivian, James Lawson, and Kelly Miller Smith—vanguard strategists in nonviolent direct action, who counseled and prepared a core of educated and motivated young students who proved ready to go to jail for their beliefs. Rev. Lawson was particularly influential, having trained in India and learned the validity of Mahatma Gandhi's philosophy of nonviolence as an instrument of social change.[32] Lawson traveled to campuses throughout the South, leading workshops for students black and white. His most basic teaching was this: "Ordinary people who acted on their conscience and took terrible risks were no longer ordinary people. They were by their very actions transformed. They would be heroes, men and women who had been abused and arrested for seeking the most elemental of human rights."[33] The students were taught how to use the tactics of passive resistance and how to respond to verbal and physical abuse (see page 16, fig. 2). Some were among the first members of their families to go to college, and they reveled in the freedom to work out a new approach to counteracting discrimination and prejudice. Among them were Diane Nash, James Bevel, and John Lewis (see page 18), all of whom started "feeling the power of an idea whose time had come"[34] and who went on to become important leaders who had a major impact on the course of the nonviolent movement.

Howard Zinn, a historian who was also active in the movement, writing in 1964 described the impact of the photographic image on the cause of student protest: "Their task is made easier by modern mass communication, for the nation, indeed the whole world, can see them on the television screen or in newspaper photos—marching, praying, singing, demonstrating their message."[35] The principal civil rights organizations—Congress of Racial Equality (CORE), The Southern Christian Leadership Conference (SCLC), and the Student Nonviolent Coordinating Committee (SNCC, commonly pronounced "snick")—were adept at employing the media to advance their goals,

Fig. 8. Bob Fletcher (American, born 1938), *SNCC Poster on a Front Porch, Ruleville, Mississippi*, 1966, gelatin silver print, 13⁷⁄₁₆ × 9 inches (34.1 × 22.8 cm), High Museum of Art, purchase with funds from Charlotte and Jim Dixon, 2007.69.

though each group independently believed that the photographs made by newspaper photographers and "outsiders" could not be relied upon to promote their causes and help raise funds to support their mission.

Of all the movement organizations, SNCC was the boldest and most progressive in its approach to media outreach, despite the fact that its membership comprised almost exclusively young, relatively inexperienced students. Its executive director, James Forman (see page 18), was savvy about publicity and had the foresight in the spring of 1962 to appoint Julian Bond (at that time an undergraduate at Morehouse College and a participant in the vigorous student-led sit-in movement in Atlanta) as SNCC's director of communications. Bond inaugurated *The Student Voice*, a newsletter that ran detailed reports on movement events, many illustrated with photographs. He was responsible for formalizing SNCC's press procedures, which included the issue of a twelve-point internal memo on the subject for its members: "It is absolutely necessary that the Atlanta office know at all times what is happening in your particular area. When action starts, the Atlanta office must be informed regularly by telephone or air mail special delivery letter so that we can issue the proper information for the press. (Atlanta has the two largest dailies in the South; we have contacts with the *New York Times*, *Newsweek*, UPI, and AP, the two wire services; we have a press list of 350 newspapers, both national and international)."[36] The same memo includes specific instructions for photographs: "Please delegate one or two people to take photographs of the action. If you have facilities to develop films *immediately* where you are, have the pictures developed and send the shots to us. If there are no facilities, send the roll(s) of film to us in manila envelopes air mail special delivery addressed personally to James Forman or Julian Bond, along with descriptions of what the photographs are about."[37]

Bond and Forman recognized that photographs, used appropriately, could be instrumental to their fundraising efforts. They also understood that the medium could be used for political gain, providing pictures for press releases and illustrations for brochures and posters (fig. 8). Photography could serve as the primary tool for documenting the movement.[38] It was Forman who recruited Danny Lyon to be SNCC's first official photographer based out of their Atlanta headquarters. Lyon, a native of New York, was just twenty years old and an undergraduate at the University of Chicago when he began working with the organization.[39] He made an immediate impact, bringing raw talent and a sense of adventure to the enterprise. In his work for SNCC he was not tied to traditional newspaper deadlines, or to any specific editorial brief, but had autonomy to choose whom and how to photograph. He was free to explore events on the ground in his own distinctive way while simultaneously absorbing the culture of the organization. He learned as he went, initially by establishing a strong rapport with Forman, for whom he served as a driver, ferrying him back and forth from meetings and demonstrations.[40] He gained Forman's trust and that of his principal colleagues, including Bond and John Lewis. Lyon became a valuable asset for SNCC and was deployed wherever his skills could be put to good use. Within this loosely structured arrangement he remained keenly aware of his role in the service of SNCC's goals: "To the watching world, SNCC was faceless. . . . My photographs were used to help create a public image."[41]

Lyon's photographs captured the day-to-day grind of marches (pl. 19) and meetings (pl. 20) as well as the frenetic, highly charged atmosphere of demonstrations and altercations that went right to the heart of the subject. In June 1963 he was dispatched to the textile town of Danville, Virginia, where police had attacked (with billy clubs and dogs) demonstrators praying at city hall. Lyon recalled that "forty-eight out of sixty-five demonstrators were injured," some severely.[42] It was the first time he had experienced the grim reality of segregated hospitals. Among the injured was Dottie Miller, a young woman who was coordinating SNCC's efforts in Danville. Lyon set to work photographing the wounded as well as the demonstrations and mass meetings that immediately followed. Within a few weeks, he and Miller had created a ten-page pamphlet documenting the violence in Danville. Miller wrote the text and Lyon provided the photographs and designed the layout. The back page of the pamphlet provides a clear statement of SNCC's mission as well as the function of such a document:

THE STUDENT NONVIOLENT COORDINATING COMMITTEE grew out of the student sit-in movement in 1960. It is composed of local protest groups across the South, a staff of 190 people, and friends of SNCC groups in the North.

SNCC staff and local affiliate group members work on voter registration and direct action in the hard core areas of the South. They daily face the violence portrayed in this pamphlet.

SNCC looks towards a day when all men shall walk with their heads high, each with equal opportunities, unafraid.

The costs of this pamphlet have been borne by SNCC in order that the Danville story could be told. Your contribution will help cover printing costs and further the struggle for human dignity in the South. Make checks payable to SNCC.[43]

Despite the hardships of a life on the road, flitting from place to place, sleeping in cars and on floors in safe houses, and putting himself in highly volatile situations, Lyon admitted: "The Danville pamphlet, a poster that makes money for SNCC, even selling pictures and passing the check on to SNCC; these things have, for a brief moment, given me a satisfaction previously unknown."[44] Lyon's work for SNCC was very effective. In the summer of 1963, a few weeks after his stint in Danville, Lyon managed to sneak up to a makeshift jail in rural southwest Georgia and take pictures of a group of teenage girls who had been arrested for demonstrating in the streets of Americus.[45] The girls were held incommunicado (some for more than a month) without charges filed against them, in a stockade several miles away from town in cramped, filthy conditions. At great personal risk, Lyon sneaked around the building, photographing the girls through the bars from outside and documenting the atrocious conditions in which they were being held—a single toilet and a dripping shower head as the only source of water. Lyon's photographs of the stockade (fig. 9) were later entered into the *Congressional Record*, providing evidence that was instrumental to securing the girls' release.

Another of Lyon's important missions for SNCC took him to Cambridge, Maryland, in the spring of 1964. There he made a shocking picture of fellow SNCC photographer Clifford Vaughs being violently apprehended by the National Guard (pl. 39).[46] Vaughs, who worked for SNCC primarily in Virginia and Maryland, looks as if he is

Fig. 9. Danny Lyon (American, born 1942), *Leesburg Stockade—Contact Sheet*, 1963, gelatin silver print, 12³⁄₁₆ × 19¹⁄₈ inches (31 × 48.6 cm), collection of the artist.

Fig. 10. George Cook (American, active 1950s–1970s), *National Guard Confronting Demonstrators, Cambridge, Maryland*, 1964, gelatin silver print, 10¹⁄₁₆ × 11⁵⁄₁₆ inches (25.5 × 28.8 cm), private collection.

being pulled limb from limb, with at least three guardsmen clutching at his clothes and legs, and a student protestor in the foreground holding onto his right ankle in a vain attempt to resist the arrest. At right foreground stands an officer, clearly of senior rank, hat in hand, staring grimly at the camera. Importantly, Lyon recollects that he made the photograph using a flash unit provided by Vaughs, who told him that he would not need it because he planned on being arrested that night.[47] Vaughs realized the publicity value of a photograph of his arrest, which could be charged with political and racial implications. His richly compelling, highly tactical form of direct action reveals the nuanced choreography underlying events that appear to be spontaneous in the photographs that record them.

A news photographer in attendance at the same episode (fig. 10) captured the unfolding action from the rooftop of the building that is pictured in the rear of Lyon's photograph. From his elevated position, George Cook, working for the *Baltimore Sun*, captured a battalion of bayonet-wielding National Guardsmen swarming around

Clifford Vaughs (1), the nearby Stokely Carmichael (2), and the watching Lyon (3), standing just a few feet away from the main action. Despite his physical proximity, Lyon seems to retain a measure of emotional distance from what is taking place, which is part of what allowed him to produce his own remarkable picture of the incident. He does not have the camera held up to his eye; rather, he seems to be intently watching the event play out in front of him. The uncanny brilliance of Lyon's photograph, which frames the action so intensely, is that it provides the viewer with the vicarious sense of what it was like to be there. He is able to convince us that he is the only photographer present, while Cook's picture establishes that this was far from the case. Besides Lyon, there are no fewer than five still photographers and two film cameramen caught in the frame.

Earlier the same night, Lyon made a striking photograph of Stokely Carmichael (pl. 40) before the young activist was felled by a particularly severe tear-gas attack. Over the course of two days and nights Lyon shot five rolls of film, intent on providing a detailed photographic record of what was happening.[48] It was difficult and dangerous work, nighttime demonstrations being especially unpredictable. As Lyon recalled: "I've never much cared for the dark, didn't own a flash, and would take pictures at night by leaning on a wall and making time exposures or by just shooting when a TV cameraman turned on his lights."[49] He adapted to the circumstances, knowing that he was there to do a job, which was to record and observe rather than to participate in the direct action. This subtle but important distinction is what distinguishes Lyon's photographs, which are at the same time persuasively objective and emotionally charged.[50]

By 1964 a separate department within SNCC—SNCC Photo—was established. SNCC Photo enlisted and trained more than a dozen photographers to actively record and document the movement. They included Tamio Wakayama, Clifford Vaughs, Joffre Clark, Rufus Hinton, Bob Fletcher (see fig. 8), Julius Lester, and Maria Varela, among others. Besides setting up darkrooms, collecting supplies, and providing publicity and documentation about the movement, SNCC Photo published pamphlets, posters, and the 1964 book *The Movement*.[51] That same year, with the support of SNCC, Matt Herron established the Southern Documentary Project to cover activities in the South during "Freedom Summer." The project, based in Mississippi, was a statewide effort to help register voters, run "Freedom Schools," set up community centers, and document areas of need and racial injustice throughout the state. Dorothea Lange served as SNCC's advisor on the project, an indication of the organization's intent to model its work on the tradition of the FSA photography of the Depression era: "SNCC Photo also documents the rural life of the South in a continuation of the work begun by Walker Evans and others under the Farm Security Administration program in the 1930s."[52]

Freedom Summer was a wide-ranging operation in which the primary civil rights organizations—SNCC, CORE, SCLC, and the NAACP—came together to form an umbrella group called the Council of Federated Organizations (COFO), with offices

Fig. 11. Bill Eppridge (American, born 1938), *Dam where bodies of Goodman, Chaney and Schwerner were found, Neshoba County, Mississippi*, August 8, 1964, gelatin silver print, 11 × 14 inches (27.9 × 35.5 cm), High Museum of Art, purchase with funds from Jeff and Valerie Levy, 2007.195.

in Columbus, Greenwood, Clarksdale, Meridian, and Hattiesburg, staffed mostly by college students who fanned out across the state in the summer of 1964. Freedom Summer got off to a horrific start with the kidnapping and disappearance of Andrew Goodman, James Chaney, and Michael Schwerner on June 21, 1964, in Philadelphia, Mississippi.[53] Goodman and Schwerner were white and from the North; Chaney was black and a native of Meridian. Attorney General Robert F. Kennedy sent the FBI and scores of federal marshals to investigate. Though the vehicle the three civil rights workers were driving was dredged from the bayou within a few days (pl. 41), it was more than a month before their bodies were found, buried in an earthen dam on the property of a noted local Klansman, Olen Burrage.[54] The FBI was led to the exact location by an informant, lured by a reward of $30,000. *Life* magazine sent photographer Bill Eppridge (and reporter Mike Murphy) to Philadelphia soon after the news broke. State authorities would not allow the two men anywhere near the crime scene, so Eppridge rented a plane to fly over the site and made aerial photographs (fig. 11). Everywhere they went, Eppridge and Murphy were followed by members of the Mississippi Sovereignty Commission, an agency created by the state legislature in 1957 to resist federal rights legislation. They established contact with the Chaney family and asked their permission to photograph the funeral and burial of their son. James Chaney was the eldest of five children, with three sisters and one brother. It was Ben Chaney, ten years old at the time, who took his brother's death the hardest. In one photograph (pl. 42) from an extensive series,[55] Eppridge eloquently captures the devastating grief and sorrow wrought on the family, as well as the lingering anger and resentment that were felt most keenly by this young boy who had lost his only brother.[56]

At Close Range

Most photographers would probably acknowledge that being in the right place at the right time trumps all skill for news stories. As the example of photographers as varied in training and background as Ernest C. Withers, Danny Lyon, Horace Cort, and Joe Postiglione has shown, having an instinctive sense of where to stand and when to click the shutter makes all the difference. One of the fascinating aspects of the civil rights movement as a photographic subject is the abundance of significant images that have

Fig. 12. Lonnie J. Wilson (American, 1924–2005), *Firemen hosing demonstrators, Kelly Ingram Park, Birmingham, Alabama*, May 3, 1963, gelatin silver print, 3½ × 4½ inches (8.9 × 11.4 cm), private collection.

Fig. 13. Bob Adelman (American, born 1930), *Kelly Ingram Park, Birmingham, Alabama*, May 3, 1963, gelatin silver print, 2⅜ × 3⁹⁄₁₆ inches (6 × 9.1 cm), collection of the artist.

been made by amateurs, many of whom used their cameras pragmatically—as a tool to record and classify information. A cache of photographs made by a detective in the Birmingham police department, Lonnie J. Wilson, shows a side of that city's richly documented civil rights history that is not commonly seen.[57] One snapshot, made from a vantage point tucked in behind a bevy of firemen (fig. 12), reveals the devastating power of the heavy fire hoses that released enough pressure to skin the bark from a tree at one hundred feet.[58] We know that established newsmen and artist photographers such as Charles Moore (pls. 31–32), Bob Adelman (pl. 28), and Bruce Davidson (pls. 29–30) were also present that day and well placed to record what happened, but none quite captured the "on top of the action" feeling conveyed by this police photographer, who was shooting from behind the lines.

Of the photographers mentioned above, Adelman perhaps comes closest.[59] His compelling picture of a lone woman desperately struggling to keep her feet and maintain her dignity while being pummeled by a white laser of water (fig. 13) was made at the edge of Kelly Ingram Park from a protected position between a police officer at left and an unknown spectator at right. Moments later, Charles Moore made several exposures of the same woman, capturing frame by frame her desperate face-off with a baton-wielding police officer (fig. 14). Of them all, it was Moore's hosing photographs that received the most media exposure. They were reproduced in an eleven-page story in *Life*, where the "slick paper and large format gave the photos a vividness and sense of enormity that newspapers couldn't touch."[60] It is Moore's eye for the individual figure that makes his photographs stand out. In one startling picture in which a woman is shown knocked to the ground by a stinging high-pressure fusillade (pl. 32), her purse wrenched from her grasp by the force of the water, the viewer shares the drenched chaos of the scene. Her fingertips alone are keeping her from falling flat, with the

Fig. 14. Charles Moore (American, born 1931), *Kelly Ingram Park, Birmingham, Alabama*, May 3, 1963, gelatin silver print, 13⅜ × 9⁵⁄₁₆ inches (34 × 23.6 cm), High Museum of Art, purchase with funds from Jess and Sherri Crawford in honor of John Lewis, 2007.248.

Fig. 15. Bill Hudson (American, active 1940s–1970s), *Police Dog Attack, Birmingham, Alabama*, May 3, 1963, gelatin silver print, 8¹⁄₁₆ × 6⅞ inches (20.4 × 17.4 cm), collection of Dan and Mary Solomon.

unmistakable glint of her wedding ring providing a jarring reminder of the commitment and sacrifice in her action. Collectively, Moore's photo story met the standards of intensity and personal accountability that one expects of a work of art. Despite its undeniable power and shock value as an ensemble, the best of Moore's photographs transcend the narrative of which they are a part.

That same day, May 3, 1963, Moore and Bill Hudson, a photographer working for the Associated Press, made some of the most important photographs of the most newsworthy episode in the entire civil rights movement—the dog attacks in Birmingham. Hudson, a former paratrooper, had sufficient experience of police hostility toward photojournalists to keep his camera (most of the time) hidden from view under his jacket, only to be brought out at the optimal moment. Hudson was there to capture the instant when a police officer grabbed the fifteen-year-old Walter Gadsden by the collar, pulling the youth toward him to provide an easy target for the attack dog at his side (fig. 15 and plate 25). Gadsden looks on, powerless to repel the dog lunging for his abdomen.[61] Standing but a few feet from his subject and using a short-range wide-angle 28mm lens, Hudson produced a photograph that brings the viewer into the heart of the action with almost brutal immediacy. The look and smell of the scene are almost palpable. The image hit the AP wire immediately and, in the professional parlance, "took the play," gaining rapid distribution; the following morning it ran on the front page of both the *New York Times* (fig. 16) and the *Washington Post*.[62] President

Fig. 16. *New York Times*, May 4, 1963, front page.

John F. Kennedy was outraged, and the photographs of Moore and Hudson were in large part the catalysts for swift federal action. These photographs and the media coverage of Birmingham had served their purpose.

In stark contrast to Hudson and Moore's inflammatory photographs of the dog attacks are photographs made by Birmingham police detective Lonnie J. Wilson. They show a much more controlled situation on the city's streets—the calm before the storm. This is the view of the demonstrations that was published in the Birmingham daily newspapers, which portrayed the police and firefighters as models of reserve. Movement historians have explained how carefully coordinated the Birmingham protests were,[63] and these photographs reveal the meticulous preparations of the police department to block off major intersections with patrol cars and motorcycles, with plainclothes officers and officials at the ready and, of course, with the canine unit on hand to control the demonstrators (figs. 17 and 18). Such photographs remain largely unpublished, either buried in police files and state archives or maintained relatively untouched in private collections.

The lead organizers of the Birmingham movement alongside Dr. King, men such as Rev. Fred Shuttlesworth and Rev. C. T. Vivian, were alert to the role that the media could play in promoting their position, and they strategically staged conflicts to draw publicity to their cause. By leading scores of well-dressed, committed, and hopeful young blacks into the streets to peacefully protest the segregation of public accommodations, where they were to be met by the defiant public safety commissioner, Eugene "Bull" Connor, only one result was likely. The leaders were able to provide undeniable evidence of the system's brutality and inequity. It was these young, proud, fearless faces—writ large in black-and-white photographic images—that transformed Dr. King's campaign and made him and his cause unstoppable.

Fig. 17. Lonnie J. Wilson (American, 1924–2005), *Police and Dogs, Birmingham, Alabama*, 1963, gelatin silver print, 3½ × 4½ inches (8.9 × 11.4 cm), private collection.

Fig. 18. Lonnie J. Wilson (American, 1924–2005), *Police Dogs and Fire Hoses, Birmingham, Alabama*, 1963, gelatin silver print, 3½ × 4½ inches (8.9 × 11.4 cm), private collection.

The violence of the South had reached into me deeper than my personal pain.

—Bruce Davidson[64]

Bruce Davidson's photographs of the civil rights movement reveal his gift for capturing the closest thing attainable to the actual event while simultaneously conjuring up the feelings associated with it. Historian Deborah Willis praises these photographs for their "layering of meaning," and their capacity to provide the viewer with a potent and nuanced view of the subject.[65] Throughout his career, Davidson has excelled in the art of photographing public moments or subjects from an intimate perspective. He works in a personal way and has stated: "I felt the need to belong when I took pictures—to discover something inside myself while making an emotional connection to my subjects."[66] While his photographs of the Birmingham water hosings (pls. 29–30) have much of the immediacy and directness of other photographs made that day, his emphasis on the desperate attempt of these youths to continue to brandish their handwritten placards in the face of the brutal onslaught adds a distinct layer of emotional power to these pictures (fig. 19 and pl. 29). Davidson is attuned to his surroundings and seems to know how and when to collaborate with the ephemeral flow of the situation in which he finds himself. His goal is always to show what the environment feels like, to demonstrate that the medium of photography can communicate emotions. As he has stated, "I'm not trying to tell a story as such, but to work around a subject intuitively, exploring different vantage points, looking for its emotional truth. If I'm looking for a story at all it's in my relationship to the subject."[67]

Fig. 19. Bruce Davidson (American, born 1933), *Kelly Ingram Park, Birmingham, Alabama*, May 3, 1963 (detail of pl. 29), gelatin silver print, 5¹⁄₁₆ × 7⁷⁄₁₆ inches (12.8 × 18.9 cm), High Museum of Art, purchase with funds from Jess and Sherri Crawford in honor of John Lewis, 2007.262.

Davidson's approach owes much to the philosophy of Henri Cartier-Bresson, whose work he studied under Ralph Hattersley at the Rochester Institute of Technology. It was Cartier-Bresson's seminal book *The Decisive Moment* (1952), which included some one hundred photographs and an accompanying text by the photographer, that transformed Davidson's thinking about himself in relation to the medium. For Cartier-Bresson the decisive moment signified that instant when the photographer "finds" himself in a picture. He said: "The discovery of oneself is made concurrently with the discovery of the world around us, but which can also be affected by us. A balance must be established between these two worlds— the one inside us and the one outside us. As a result of a constant reciprocal process, both these worlds come together to form a single one."[68] For his part, Davidson seems to understand that, despite frequent claims to the contrary, photography has never been a medium especially suited to storytelling. Isolating single fragments out of the continuity of time—which is what photographs do—is counter to the idea of narrative. Davidson's photographs, at their best, subvert the narrative idea and instead describe the look and feel of an experience, memorializing the quality of a particular moment (see pls. 18, 24, 29, 30).

Foot Soldiers

The elevation of Dr. King to iconic status as a civil rights leader has partially obscured the courageous and determined efforts of thousands of ordinary people who participated in and contributed to the movement. Gifted and dedicated local organizers throughout the South were the backbone of the movement, and they made it possible for Dr. King and other leaders to transform what was considered a local issue into a national crisis that merited international attention.[69] While the movement's formal leadership may have come from businesses, churches, and national organizations, it was mostly private citizens—many of them women—who played prominent roles in organizing effectively for change. One such important grassroots leader was Septima Clark, who taught for forty years in the South Carolina school system before she was summarily dismissed in 1956 for refusing to relinquish her NAACP membership. Clark successfully campaigned to allow African Americans to teach in Charleston and earn pay equivalent to their white counterparts. In the 1950s she regularly taught workshops at the Highlander Folk School on the tactics required to advance school desegregation, voter registration, and leadership in education.[70] In 1961 she was recruited by Dr. King and the SCLC to serve as director of education and teaching, a role that required her to carry out citizenship training, voter registration, and literacy programs.

Similarly influential was Fannie Lou Hamer (see pls. 52–53), the twentieth child born to a family of sharecroppers in Montgomery County in the heart of the Mississippi Delta. She knew firsthand the impoverished conditions of blacks in the South, and it was her strong desire to improve those conditions that fueled her activism. She worked with SNCC, predominantly in her home state, dedicating herself to voter registration. When she tried to register to vote, she lost her job as a plantation worker and was brutally beaten and arrested on several occasions. The spirit of Hamer's radical voice is captured in her autobiography, *To Praise Our Bridges*, which was published by SNCC: "What I really feel is necessary is that the black people in this country will have to upset the applecart. We can no longer ignore the fact that America is NOT the '. . . land of the free and the home of the brave.' I used to question this for years—what did our kids actually fight for? They would go in the service and go through all of that and come right out and be drowned in the river in Mississippi."[71] It was Hamer's emotional testimony before the Credentials Committee of the 1964 Democratic National Convention that helped bring the crimes inflicted on blacks seeking the right to vote in her home state to a national audience.[72]

The examples of Clark and Hamer greatly inspired another young educator and activist, Doris Derby, who studied anthropology at the University of Illinois and sought to establish vibrant local organizations capable of responding to conditions in the rural South. A native of New York, Derby became involved in civil rights action in the summer of 1962, when she traveled to Albany, Georgia, to visit a friend who had been arrested there for demonstrating.[73] After spending the summer going back and forth between Albany and Atlanta, during which time she worked with James Forman, Septima Clark, and Dr. King, Derby returned to New York and became a founding member of SNCC's office there. She proved able and resourceful. Derby staged several fundraising events that brought much-needed dollars to the organization. For one such effort she invited Bob Moses, the de facto leader of SNCC's efforts in Mississippi. Moses suggested that Derby move south to help implement an experimental adult literacy program, which she did at Tougaloo College. She developed instructional materials and methods to prepare black men and women to take the literacy test required to gain voting rights.

Having studied painting as an undergraduate, Doris Derby had a background in the visual arts and firmly believed in the power of creative endeavors to raise the consciousness of black people, in both education and employment. She attended the first meeting of the Poor People's Corporation at Tougaloo College on August 29, 1965, the main

Fig. 20. Doris Derby (American, born 1939), *Volunteer Math Teacher, Mound Bayou, Mississippi*, 1968, gelatin silver print, 9⅜ × 13¹⁵⁄₁₆ inches (23.8 × 35.4 cm), High Museum of Art, purchase with funds from Jeff and Valerie Levy, 2007.191.

purpose of which was to assist low-income groups in their efforts to initiate and sustain self-help projects of a cooperative nature. These projects were designed to ameliorate the effects of poverty. Derby was also intimately involved with an offshoot agency of the Poor People's Corporation called Southern Media, Inc., based in Jackson, Mississippi. Its staff coached media and communication skills to black community groups—which included training in the use of still and movie cameras—with the goal of enabling those living in isolated rural areas to document their own lives and communities.[74] It was in this environment that Derby first practiced and taught photography.

Derby was largely self-taught in the medium and used her camera primarily to document the role of women in the movement such as L. C. Dorsey, who worked with the Southern Coalition on Jails and Prisons and the Mississippi Council on Human Relations.[75] Dorsey founded the North Bolivar County Farm Cooperative (pl. 57) to encourage subsistence farming and vocational training for women who had been dismissed from their jobs (mostly as maids and housekeepers in white homes) because they registered to vote. Derby's study of a volunteer math teacher in Mound Bayou, Mississippi (fig. 20), is typical of the kind of picture she made, melding her passion for community activism with a desire to record a social fabric that was largely ignored by the mainstream media.

Morton Broffman, a passionate and skilled amateur photographer, gave up his profession as a teacher in the mid-1950s to pursue a career as a freelance photographer.[76] He worked for Senator Hubert Humphrey in 1960 and served as a presidential campaign photographer for Eugene McCarthy in 1968.[77] A committed Democrat and liberal who naturally gravitated toward social causes, Broffman dedicated himself to documenting with his camera some of the key events and gatherings of the civil rights era. In addition to several major publications, Broffman also worked for *The Cathedral Age* magazine of the Washington National Cathedral for more than twenty-five years until his death in 1992. In that capacity he photographed many politicians and public figures as well as

Fig. 21. Morton Broffman (American, 1928–1992), *Selma to Montgomery March, Alabama,* 1965, gelatin silver print, 13¹¹⁄₁₆ × 10⁹⁄₁₆ inches (34.7 × 26.8 cm), High Museum of Art, gift of the Broffman family, 2007.52.

demonstrations and marches in the nation's capital.[78] He was one of scores of photographers from around the country who traveled to Alabama to participate in and record the Selma to Montgomery March for Voting Rights in the spring of 1965.

The fifty-four miles from Selma to Montgomery along Highway 80 in Alabama took marchers five days to complete. It was the largest civil rights demonstration the state had ever seen. Many who had never participated in the movement walked side by side with those who had been demonstrating for a decade. By the final leg of the march the number had swelled to some twenty-five to thirty thousand people. Almost every important news organization had reporters, photographers, and camera crews on the ground in Alabama, with personnel who were experienced in press coverage.[79] Broffman made dozens of photographs along the route. He did his best work on the final day, when Dr. King led several thousand marchers into the heart of Montgomery up Dexter Avenue (pl. 76), past the Baptist church that had been his congregation during the Montgomery Bus Boycott, to the steps of the state capitol. This was the very building where George Wallace was sworn in as governor in 1963, vowing to keep Alabama segregated forever. As the crowds settled into position for the rally and speeches, Broffman captured the excitement and expectation of the assembled marchers as well as the fatigue and exhaustion brought on by five days on foot in difficult, damp conditions (see pl. 74).

Alongside Dr. King were several of the heroes of the movement, among them Rosa Parks, Roy Wilkins of the NAACP, John Lewis of SNCC, and Whitney Young of the National Urban League. Among the celebrities were writer James Baldwin and singer Joan Baez (pl. 66). Morton Broffman produced affecting portraits of many of them. He seems to have learned that the audience could be as compelling a subject as the main event. His pictures of children milling around in the crowd, watching, waiting, and listening to the speeches (pls. 77–78), are especially tender and intimate. Their faces are full of emotion and expectation, and of course their participation offered hope and the possibility that real and meaningful change may have finally come. In more than one photograph, Broffman singled out the children of Rev. Ralph Abernathy (fig. 21), who

Fig. 22. Unknown photographer, *Ku Klux Klan Convoy on Rural Highway*, ca. 1960–1965, gelatin silver print, 3¹⁄₁₆ × 5½ inches (7.7 × 13.9 cm), collection of Emory University, Manuscript, Archives, and Rare Book Library.

were there to witness this historic march on the Alabama state capitol. As one eight-year-old marcher, Sheyann Webb, remembered: "It was like we *had* overcome. We had reached the point we had been fighting for, for a long time. . . . And if you were to just stand there in the midst of thousands and thousands of people and all the great leaders and political people who had come from all over the world, it was just a thrill. I asked my mother and father for my birthday present to become registered voters. They took me to the polls with them to vote."[80]

The photography of the civil rights movement includes the work of great photographers but also simple and powerful images by photographers of modest aspiration and small renown. Sometimes the maker's identity is unknown. These anonymous photographers have the occasional eye for the telling image, and by virtue of sheer numbers and their obvious industry their work warrants and repays study.

Standing in the middle of a nameless rural back road (fig. 22), one anonymous shutterbug, whose ideological beliefs would appear to be glaringly transparent, reminds us of how coherent and laser-like the camera can be in its articulation of time and space. The viewer is shuttled back in time to a scene of the kind that was responsible for taking hundreds of innocent lives. The window that photography justly claims to provide on the world also firmly demarcates our separation from that world. The French cultural critic Roland Barthes makes much of what he refers to as photography's "umbilical" connection to its subject.[81] According to Barthes, the reality offered by the photograph is not so much its truth-to-appearance as its truth-to-presence. The transcriptive and suggestive power of the photograph allows it to transcend mere resemblance and conjure a "subject"—to provide what Barthes calls a "certificate of presence."[82] This particular snapshot reminds us that some photographs of the civil rights era—no matter the circumstances of their production—are stamped with a disquieting, lingering aura that cannot be ignored. This is a medium that does best with things that are vanishing and which, we can only hope, no contrivance on earth can bring back again.

Notes

1. Langston Hughes, *Selected Poems of Langston Hughes* (New York: Alfred A. Knopf, 1989), 268. Also quoted in W. Haywood Burns, *The Voices of Negro Protest in America* (London and New York: Oxford University Press, 1963), 61.

2. Steven Kasher, *The Civil Rights Movement: A Photographic History, 1954–1968* (New York: Abbeville Press, 1996), 17. I am deeply grateful to Kasher, not only for his scholarship and knowledge of the subject, but for his goodwill and support of this project. He brought to my attention many important and rare civil rights photographs that are now part of the permanent collection of the High Museum of Art.

3. This phrase was used repeatedly by Charlie Kelly, staff photographer for the Associated Press from 1961 to 1970, initially in Memphis, then Milwaukee, and from 1966 in Atlanta. The same phrasing is also used in Kasher, 12.

4. Author interview with Moses Newson, January 22, 2008. See also Gene Roberts and Hank Klibanoff, *The Race Beat: The Press, the Civil Rights Struggle, and the Awakening of a Nation* (New York: Alfred A. Knopf, 2006), 95–96, 165–166, 176–178.

5. Author interview with Charles Moore, October 17, 2007. See also Roberts and Klibanoff, 316–319.

6. Lonnie Joe Wilson was a lifetime law enforcement officer for the Birmingham police department. Wilson joined the department shortly after World War II and served with distinction for more than thirty years. During the civil rights era, Detective Wilson was assigned to several details that required him to be involved with the planning and coordination of crowd control and logistics associated with protests and marches in Birmingham. Frequently, Wilson was required to escort civil rights leaders for their safety and protection. The existence of this photograph (and others by Wilson) was kindly brought to my attention by Paul Conlan, who put me in touch with the owners. The photographs are the property of Vicki Wilson Hunt and her two siblings, Greg Wilson and Marsha Wilson.

7. For a detailed discussion of the Till murder and trial, see Roberts and Klibanoff, 86–108 and Juan Williams, *Eyes on the Prize, America's Civil Rights Years, 1954–1965* (New York: Penguin Books, 2002, revised ed.), 38–57.

8. Roberts and Klibanoff, 88, 265.

9. Withers also made important civil rights photographs of the desegregation of Central High School in Little Rock, Arkansas, in 1957, and James Meredith's admission to the University of Mississippi in 1962. For details, see Michele Furst, Ronald W. Bailey, and Ernest C. Withers, *Let Us March On! Selected Civil Rights Photographs of Ernest C. Withers* (Boston: Massachusetts College of Art, 1992) and Ernest C. Withers, Jack F. Hurley, Brooks Johnson, and Daniel J. Wolff, *Pictures Tell the Story: Ernest C. Withers, Reflections in History* (Norfolk, Virginia: Chrysler Museum of Art, 2000). See also Hank Klibanoff's obituary and appreciation of Withers, "The Eye on the Prize," in *The New York Times Magazine*, December 30, 2007, 44–45.

10. The typical transmission time was 5–7 minutes per image.

11. Roberts and Klibanoff, 321. They also make the point that television ownership allowed blacks "to view contemporary entertainment without having to suffer the ignominy of trudging up to an isolated balcony at the movie theater."

12. *Eyes on the Prize*, 270, and Kasher, 12.

13. An exception to this rule was Kathryn Johnson, who in 1964 became the first female reporter to be employed in the Atlanta AP bureau. She worked there alongside photographers Charlie Kelly and Horace Cort. In 1966, Bob Johnson, a schoolteacher who moonlighted for the *Atlanta Inquirer*, became the first African American staff photographer appointed in the Atlanta AP bureau. For more on Kathryn Johnson's career, see *Breaking News: How the Associated Press Has Covered War, Peace and Everything Else*, Reporters of the Associated Press with a Foreword by David Halberstam (New York: Princeton Architectural Press, 2007), 320–323.

14. *Graphic*, June 13, 1963, 11. This local weekly newspaper published in Tuscaloosa, Alabama, includes a photograph of a news photographer improvising an outdoor darkroom while covering Governor George Wallace's stand to deny two black students, Vivian Malone and James Hood, entry to the University of Alabama in June 1963. I am grateful to Hank Klibanoff for sharing an offprint of the newspaper with me.

15. See also *Breaking News*, 198.

16. Brian Coe, *Cameras, From Daguerreotypes to Instant Pictures* (New York: Crown Publishers, 1978), 50, 232. See also *http://graflex.org/speed-graphic*. AP photographer Charlie Kelly recalls that he and his fellow photographers were advised on more than one occasion by Claude Sitton, who covered the civil rights beat for the *New York Times*, to scale down their equipment. Sitton implored reporters and news photographers alike to be as unobtrusive as possible when working on civil rights stories. Author interview with Charlie Kelly, November 11, 2007.

17. See *Breaking News*, 197.

18. Atlanta History Center, Herbert Jenkins Archive. A July 3, 1964, police report drafted by Sergeant M. G. Redding for the Atlanta Chief of Police, Herbert Jenkins, stated that a number of Ku Klux Klansmen and members of the National States' Rights Party were present that day in support of Maddox's stand. The Klansmen included Calvin F. Craig, grand wizard of Georgia.

19. Maddox drew publicity for his resistance in the *Atlanta Journal*, July 4 and 7, 1964, and the *New York Times*, August 12 and 14, 1964, September 30, 1964, and February 2, 8, and 23, 1965.

20. Atlanta History Center, MS 546, Box 18, Folder 3, unidentified newspaper clipping.

21. Emory University MS 629, *The White American*, October 1964, a white supremacist journal published in Birmingham, ran a front-page story in support of Maddox and his stand over his restaurant. See also Jason Sokol, *There Goes My Everything, White Southerners in the Age of Civil Rights, 1945–1975* (New York: Alfred A. Knopf, 2006), 183–187.

22. A story in the *New York Times*, September 28, 1964, reported that Maddox turned away the same three young men (and another named Charles Wells) for trying to enter his re-named restaurant, the Lester Maddox Cafeteria.

23. Quoted in *The Heretics*, Summer 1966, 17, in an article by Lester Maddox titled "I Closed My Shop When I Was Ordered to Serve Negroes," Getty Research Institute, Charles Brittin Archive, Box 46.

24. For an excellent history of the Freedom Rides, see Raymond Arsenault, *Freedom Riders: 1961 and the Struggle for Racial Justice* (New York: Oxford University Press, 2006).

25. Ibid., 140–148, where the attack is described in detail. See also Roberts and Klibanoff, 242–245.

26. Roberts and Klibanoff, 245, 248.

27. A cache of sixty-four photographs by Postiglione was donated to the Birmingham Civil Rights Institute in December 2005 by the Anniston law firm of Merrill, Merrill, Matthews and Allen, LLC. Postiglione's photographs were part of the evidence submitted in the criminal case brought against six men who faced federal charges for setting fire to the bus. Postiglione also testified at the trial, which ended in a hung jury. There was no second trial. The men pleaded guilty to lesser charges and were placed on probation. I am most grateful to Fred Burger, a freelance writer based in Anniston, Alabama, for sharing this information.

28. *Anniston Star*, May 15, 1961, front page, 10. Again, I am grateful to Fred Burger for sharing this reference with me and to Hank Klibanoff for connecting me with Mr. Burger.

29. Postiglione left Anniston in 1962 and moved to Kentucky, where he worked for Hollywood Studio in Owensboro. His obituary in the *Owensboro Messenger Inquirer*, October 17, 1995, 2C, said that he had been "a photographer for 40 years before his retirement."

30. Arsenault, 145–146.

31. Hughes, *Selected Poems*, 280.

32. David Halberstam, *The Children* (New York: Random House, 1998), 47–49, and *Eyes on the Prize*, 123.

33. Halberstam, 62.

34. Diane Nash, quoted in *Eyes on the Prize*, 129.

35. Howard Zinn, *SNCC: The New Abolitionists* (Boston: Beacon Press, 1964), 7–8.

36. Emory University Special Collections, Constance Curry Papers, MS 818, Box 3, Folder 1.

37. Ibid.

38. Roberts and Klibanoff, 312. By 1963–1964 SNCC had appointed at least two traveling photographers and had a fully equipped darkroom and storage area for photographs in their Atlanta offices. See also Julian Bond in the foreword to Danny Lyon, *Memories*, 6.

39. Lyon's role in the movement and his work for SNCC are richly documented in his own publication, *Memories of the Civil Rights Movement* (Chapel Hill: University of North Carolina Press, 1992).

40. Author interview with Danny Lyon, November 6, 2007.

41. Lyon, *Memories*, 30.

42. Ibid., 63. See pp. 62–69 for a full description of Lyon's work in Danville, Virginia.

43. Emory University Library Special Collections, Constance Curry Papers, MS 818, Box 3, Folder 3. SNCC Danville Brochure, published August 1963.

44. Lyon, *Memories*, 135. The quote is from a letter Lyon wrote to his mother (reproduced in full) on February 12, 1964.

45. Ibid., 78–81.

46. In the fall of 1964, Vaughs was again beaten and his equipment destroyed in Philadelphia, Mississippi. See SNCC Photo (Organizational Brochure), Museum of Modern Art Archives, New York.

47. See Lyon, *Memories*, 136.

48. In Lyon's negative filing system the story number is 62-17-1.

49. Lyon, *Memories*, 136.

50. Nathan Lyons was perhaps the first curator and writer to recognize this duality in Lyon's work. He included Lyon's photographs in his 1966 exhibition *Toward a Social Landscape* at the George Eastman House in Rochester, New York. The work of Lee Friedlander, Garry Winogrand, and Bruce Davidson was included, among others. Lyons was interested in work that represented photography's nonliteral qualities, and he wanted to "recognize the significance of photography on idiographic terms, as representing ideas and providing illustrations for words." Lyons, *Toward a Social Landscape* (New York: Horizon Press, 1967), n.p.

51. *The Movement*, 1964, included the work of more than fifteen photographers, many of whom have become important figures in the history of the medium, such as Danny Lyon, Robert Frank, Roy De Carava, Bob Adelman, and Matt Herron. The title page of the publication includes the following statement: "This book was prepared with the cooperation and assistance of the Student Nonviolent Coordinating Committee." In addition to this publication, SNCC Photo also organized the 1965

exhibition *NOW* and the 1967 exhibition *US*, presented at the Countee Cullen Library, Harlem, in 1967. An archive of more than 150 contact sheets and work prints, by several of the SNCC photographers mentioned in this essay, is part of the Photographs and Prints Division at the Schomburg Center for Research in Black Culture, New York Public Library.

52. SNCC Photo (Organizational Brochure), Museum of Modern Art Archives, New York. My thanks to Erina Duganne and Jennifer Tobias for sharing this reference with me.

53. Roberts and Klibanoff, 353–364, and *Eyes on the Prize*, 231–235.

54. During the search for the bodies, the FBI and federal marshals found the bodies of seven other African Americans in the same vicinity.

55. Eppridge's photo essay comprises more than sixty photographs. A story on the discovery of the bodies ran in *Life*, August 14, 1964. A variant of this particular aerial photograph was reproduced with that story. On June 21, 2005, exactly 21 years after the murders, Edgar Ray Killen was convicted of manslaughter in the deaths of Chaney, Goodman, and Schwerner. Others involved in the crime have never been convicted.

56. *Life*, June 19, 1970, 38–39. The magazine ran this picture six years later in an article titled "The Two Nightmares of Ben Chaney," by Michael Mok. Chaney faced murder charges in South Carolina for the murder of three white men in Florida. He was convicted and served a thirteen-year sentence.

57. See note 6. This cache of photographs comprises more than thirty prints, of which eight were generously loaned to the High Museum of Art for further research and study.

58. Taylor Branch, *Parting the Waters: America in the King Years, 1954–1963* (New York: Simon and Schuster Inc., 1988), 759. See also Roberts and Klibanoff, 316.

59. Bruce Davidson, relatively small in stature, remembers "hiding" behind the much bigger Bob Adelman that day, using him as a shield of sorts during the thick of the action. The two photographers also worked side by side later that day, making photographs of demonstrators being arrested outside the Loveman's department store in Birmingham (see pls. 23–24). Davidson described the same pattern when they were both covering the Selma to Montgomery March in 1965. Author interview with Bruce Davidson, May 22, 2007.

60. Roberts and Klibanoff, 322.

61. Ibid., 318. The authors state that Gadsden was a member of the Scott family of Atlanta, who owned both the *Atlanta Daily World* and the *Birmingham World* newspapers, both of which were consistent critics of Dr. King. It was ironic, then, that Gadsden became the poster child for the success of King's youth crusade in Birmingham.

62. Ibid., 318–319.

63. Ibid., 316–333, and Branch, 756–802.

64. Quoted in *Bruce Davidson Photography* (New York: Agrine Publications and Summit Books, 1978), 12.

65. Deborah Willis in *Time of Change—Bruce Davidson Civil Rights Photographs 1961–1965* (Los Angeles: St. Ann's Press, 2002), n.p.

66. Quoted in *Bruce Davidson Photography*, 9.

67. Quoted in *Magnum Stories*, ed. Chris Boot (London and New York: Phaidon, 2004), 90. A good example of Davidson's ability to examine the nuanced aspects of a subject are the photographs that illustrated a story by Claude Brown titled "The Power of Blackness," in *Look*, June 27, 1967, 22–32.

68. Henri Cartier Bresson, *The Decisive Moment* (New York: Simon and Schuster, 1952), n.p.

69. Julian Bond's introduction in *Eyes on the Prize*, IX–XV. This publication (and film) was the first major corrective in this regard.

70. See Grace Jordan McFadden, "Septima P. Clark and the Struggle for Human Rights," in *Women in the Civil Rights Movement: Trailblazers and Torchbearers 1941–1965*, Vicki L. Crawford, Jacqueline Anne Rouse, and Barbara Woods, eds. (Bloomington & Indianapolis: Indiana University Press, 1990), 85–98.

71. Fannie Lou Hamer, *To Praise Our Bridges* (Jackson, Mississippi: Kipco Publishing and Student Nonviolent Coordinating Committee, 1967), 15. The publication is illustrated with photographs by SNCC photographers Julius Lester and Maria Varela. See also *Eyes on the Prize*, 245–247, which includes an excerpt from Hamer's autobiography.

72. For more on Fannie Lou Hamer, see *Eyes on the Prize*, 241–247, and Mamie E. Locke, "Is This America? Fannie Lou Hamer and the Mississippi Freedom Democratic Party," in Crawford, Rouse, and Woods, eds., 27–38.

73. Clarissa Myrick-Harris, "Behind the Scenes: Doris Derby, Denise Nicholas and the Free Southern Theater," in Crawford, Rouse, and Woods, eds., 219–224.

74. Emory University, MS 935, Doris Derby Papers, Box 1 —Southern Media pamphlet. Another photographer who was heavily involved in similar initiatives in Mississippi was Julius Lester, who helped establish Flute Publications (organized and funded by the Poor People's Corporation), dedicated to publishing the prose and poetry of poor rural blacks.

75. Ibid., Box 1. L. C. Dorsey's background and vocational goals are described in the pamphlet "Freedom Come to Mississippi."

76. Broffman was born in the Bronx, New York, in 1928. After graduating from DeWitt Clinton High School, he studied history and political science at Rutgers University. He attended New York University Law School until he was drafted into the army. It was after military service that he took up a career in teaching, working for many years

at the Georgetown Day School in Washington and later at the Wakefield High School in Arlington, Virginia.

77. Broffman was for many years involved with a group called *Americans for Democratic Action*, and it was through his association with this organization that he came to work for Senator Humphrey. He photographed Humphrey extensively. Four of Broffman's portraits of Humphrey (including the cover image) were reproduced in a publication by Michael Amrine, *This is Humphrey: The Story of the Senator* (Garden City, New York: Doubleday & Company, Inc., 1960).

78. Broffman's photographs of the Poor People's Campaign and Resurrection City, which took place in Washington in May and June 1968, are especially good and are an important document of that event.

79. The march was extensively covered in the African American press. Simeon Booker's story "50,000 March on Montgomery" was published in the May 1965 issue of *Ebony*, with more than 95 photographs by Moneta Sleet Jr. and Maurice Sorrell, among others.

80. Quoted in Henry Hampton and Steven Fayer, *Voices of Freedom: An Oral History of the Civil Rights Movement from the 1950s through the 1980s* (New York: Bantam Books, 1991), 240.

81. Roland Barthes, *Camera Lucida: Reflections on Photography*, trans. Richard Howard (New York: Hill and Wang, 1981), 81.

82. Ibid., 85.

Plates

1. Dan Weiner (American, 1919–1959)

Dr. Martin Luther King Jr. Addressing a Mass Meeting at First Baptist Church,

Montgomery, Alabama, 1956

2. Unknown Photographer (*New York Times*)

Rosa Parks Being Fingerprinted, Montgomery, Alabama, February 22, 1956

3. Ernest C. Withers (American, 1922–2007)

First Desegregated Bus Ride, Montgomery, Alabama, 1956

4. Charles Moore (American, born 1931)

Dr. Martin Luther King Jr. Arrested, Montgomery, Alabama, 1958

5. Unknown Photographer (*New York Times*)

Elizabeth Eckford Entering Central High School, Little Rock, Arkansas, September 5, 1957

6. Will Counts (American, 1931–1995)

L. Alex Wilson, Reporter for the *Tri-State Defender*, Memphis, Attacked by a Crowd,

Central High School, Little Rock, Arkansas, September 23, 1957

7. Unknown Photographer (Associated Press)

John Lewis and Jim Zwerg Beaten, Montgomery, Alabama, May 20, 1961

(BM2)BIRMINGHAM, Ala., May 20—ANOTHER BUS CANCELED—Greyhound driver Joe Cavanaugh
stands at the door of his bus in Birmingham today and tells a group of "freedom riders"
attempting to board that the trip has been canceled. "I have only one life to give and
I don't intend to give it for CORE and the NAACP," Cavanaugh told the racially mixed
group which renewed integration efforts after a night of waiting at the station.
(AP Wirephoto) (JL70735stf-hwc) 1961   See AP Wire Story

8. Horace Cort (American, active 1940s–1970s)

Another Bus Cancelled, Birmingham, Alabama, May 20, 1961

55

9. Unknown Photographer (Associated Press)

National Guardsman, Montgomery Bus Station, Alabama, May 22, 1961

10. Bob Adelman (American, born 1930)

CORE Freedom Ride Bus, Westminster, Maryland, 1963

11. Donald Blumberg (American, born 1935)

Bus Rider, Mobilization for Youth, March on Washington, D.C., 1963

12. Unknown Photographer (United Press International)

Winston Henry Lockett and Alfred David Jones Jr., Wake County Jail, Raleigh,

North Carolina, August 15, 1962

13. Unknown Photographer (*New York Times*)

Members of SNCC Praying at Burned-out Church, Dawson, Georgia, September 9, 1962

14. Consuelo Kanaga (American, 1894–1978)

Peace and Freedom Walkers, Albany, Georgia, 1962

15. Danny Lyon (American, born 1942)

A Terminal in the Delta, Clarksdale, Mississippi, 1962

16. Bob Adelman (American, born 1930)

Ferry across the Mississippi River, near Plaquemine, Louisiana, 1964

17. Steve Schapiro (American, born 1936)

"Segregation Forever," Fort Lauderdale, Florida, 1964

18. Bruce Davidson (American, born 1933)

Ku Klux Klan Rally, Atlanta, Georgia, 1962

19. Danny Lyon (American, born 1942)

Atlanta, Georgia, 1963

20. Danny Lyon (American, born 1942)

SNCC Office Staff, Atlanta, Georgia, 1963

21. Horace Cort (American, active 1940s–1970s)

Man Spraying Deodorant over Heads of Sit-in Demonstrators at Woolworth's,

Atlanta, Georgia, October 20, 1960

22. Unknown Photographer (*New York Times*)

Civil Rights Demonstrators and Ku Klux Klan Members Share the Same Sidewalk,

Atlanta, Georgia, January 25, 1964

23. Bob Adelman (American, born 1930)

Picketers Arrested behind Loveman's Department Store, Birmingham, Alabama, May 1963

24. Bruce Davidson (American, born 1933)

Arresting Demonstrators, Birmingham, Alabama, May 1963

25. Bill Hudson (American, active 1940s–1970s)

Police Dog Attack, Birmingham, Alabama, May 3, 1963

26. Unknown Photographer (*New York Times*)

Electric Cattle Prod, June 21, 1963

27. Unknown Photographer (Associated Press)

Firemen Hosing Demonstrators, Kelly Ingram Park, Birmingham, Alabama, May 3, 1963

28. Bob Adelman (American, born 1930)

Firemen Hosing Demonstrators, Kelly Ingram Park, Birmingham, Alabama, May 3, 1963

29. Bruce Davidson (American, born 1933)

Kelly Ingram Park, Birmingham, Alabama, May 3, 1963

30. Bruce Davidson (American, born 1933)

Kelly Ingram Park, Birmingham, Alabama, May 3, 1963

31. Charles Moore (American, born 1931)

Kelly Ingram Park, Birmingham, Alabama, May 3, 1963

32. Charles Moore (American, born 1931)

Kelly Ingram Park, Birmingham, Alabama, May 3, 1963

33. Moneta Sleet, Jr. (American, 1926–1996)

Dr. Martin Luther King in the Midst, March on Washington, D.C., 1963

34. Danny Lyon (American, born 1942)

John Lewis, March on Washington, D.C., 1963

35. Builder Levy (American, born 1942)

March on Washington, D.C., 1963

36. Declan Haun (American, 1937–1994)

Picketing the Courthouse, Monroe, North Carolina, August 26, 1961

37. Declan Haun (American, 1937–1994)

Dr. Martin Luther King Jr. Arriving at the 16th Street Baptist Church,

Birmingham, Alabama, 1963

38. Declan Haun (American, 1937–1994)

16th Street Baptist Church, Birmingham, Alabama, 1963

39. Danny Lyon (American, born 1942)

SNCC Photographer Clifford Vaughs is Arrested by the National Guard,

Cambridge, Maryland, 1964

40. Danny Lyon (American, born 1942)

Stokely Carmichael, Confrontation with National Guard, Cambridge, Maryland, 1964

41. Steve Schapiro (American, born 1936)

The Civil Rights Workers' Station Wagon, Philadelphia, Mississippi, 1964

42. Bill Eppridge (American, born 1938)

Chaney Family as They Depart for the Funeral of James Chaney, Philadelphia, Mississippi, 1964

43. Declan Haun (American, 1937–1994)

Voting Booth, Alabama, 1965

44. Bob Adelman (American, born 1930)

Box in Frank Robinson's CORE Voter Registration Office, Sumter, South Carolina, 1962

45. Bob Adelman (American, born 1930)

Prospective Voter Studies Sample Voter Registration Form in CORE Office,

Sumter, South Carolina, 1962

46. Bob Adelman (American, born 1930)

Woman Registering to Vote, Sumter, South Carolina, 1962

47. James Kerlin (American, active 1940s–1970s)

Cleaning the Pool, St. Augustine, Florida, June 18, 1964

48. Unknown Photographer

Dr. Martin Luther King Jr. and Rev. Ralph Abernathy, John's County Jail,

St. Augustine, Florida, 1964

49. Declan Haun (American, 1937–1994)

Man Praying, Selma, Alabama, 1965

50. Bob Adelman (American, born 1930)

Woman Being Arrested, Downstate Medical Center, Brooklyn, New York, 1963

51. Bob Adelman (American, born 1930)

Dr. Martin Luther King Jr., Camden, Alabama, 1966

52. Marvin Roth (American, active 1940s–1970s)

Fannie Lou Hamer, ca. 1964

53. Steve Schapiro (American, born 1936)

Fannie Lou Hamer at Home, Ruleville, Mississippi, 1963

54. Bob Fitch (American, born 1939)

Dr. Martin Luther King Jr. in the SCLC Office, Atlanta, Georgia, 1966

55. Gordon Parks (American, 1912–2006)

Muslim Boy Selling Newspapers, 1963

56. Leonard Freed (American, 1929–2006)

CORE Demonstration, Brooklyn, New York, 1963

57. Doris Derby (American, born 1939)

L. C. Dorsey, Civil Rights Worker from Shelby, Mississippi, at the Vegetable Cooperative,

Ruleville, Mississippi, 1968

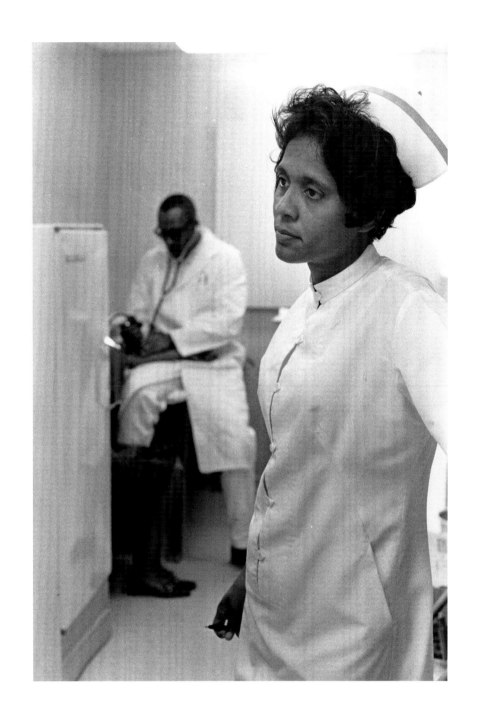

58. Doris Derby (American, born 1939)

Nurse and Doctor, Health Clinic in the Mississippi Delta, 1968

59. Unknown Photographer (*New York Times*)

Protestors against Dallas County Sheriff Jim Clark and Segregation, Selma, Alabama, 1965

60. Declan Haun (American, 1937–1994)

Caricature of Sheriff Jim Clark and a Drawing of Dr. Martin Luther King Jr. Posted on a Wall,

Selma, Alabama, 1965

61. James "Spider" Martin (American, 1939–2003)

State Trooper Gives Marchers "Two Minute Warning," Selma, Alabama, March 7, 1965

62. James "Spider" Martin (American, 1939–2003)

Amelia Boynton Beaten by State Troopers, Selma, Alabama, March 7, 1965

63. Unknown Photographer

State Troopers Break Up Marchers, Selma, Alabama, March 7, 1965

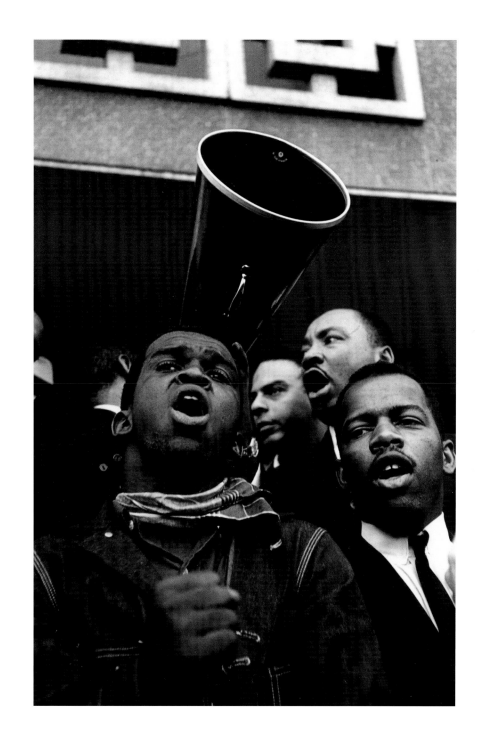

64. Steve Schapiro (American, born 1936)

Andrew Young, Martin Luther King Jr., and John Lewis, Selma, Alabama, 1965

65. Charles Moore (American, born 1931)

Freedom Singing, Selma, Alabama, 1965

112

66. Matt Herron (American, born 1931)

James Baldwin, Joan Baez, and James Forman, Selma to Montgomery March, Alabama, 1965

67. Matt Herron (American, born 1931)

Selma to Montgomery March, Alabama, 1965

68. Moneta Sleet, Jr. (American, 1926–1996)

Marchers on the Road to Montgomery, Alabama, 1965

69. James H. Karales (American, 1930–2002)

Bystanders, Selma to Montgomery March, Alabama, 1965

70. Declan Haun (American, 1937–1994)

Children in the Crowd, Selma, Alabama, 1965

71. Ivan Massar (American, born 1924)

Dr. Martin Luther King Jr., Coretta Scott King, John Lewis, and Others,

Selma to Montgomery March, Alabama, 1965

72. Moneta Sleet, Jr. (American, 1926–1996)

Dr. King and Coretta Scott King Singing in the Rain, Selma to Montgomery March, Alabama, 1965

73. Steve Schapiro (American, born 1936)

Boy with American Flag, Selma to Montgomery March, Alabama, 1965

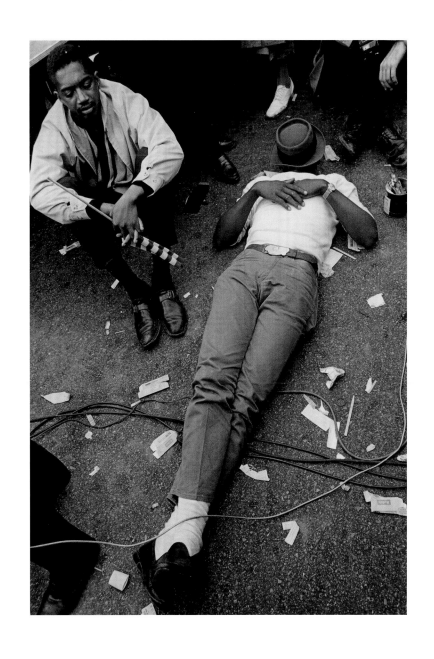

74. Morton Broffman (American, 1928–1992)

Conclusion of the Selma to Montgomery March, Alabama, 1965

75. Steve Schapiro (American, born 1936)

Andrew Young, Rev. Ralph Abernathy, and Dr. Martin Luther King Jr.,

Selma to Montgomery March, Alabama, 1965

76. Morton Broffman (American, 1928–1992)

Dr. King and Coretta Scott King Leading Marchers, Montgomery, Alabama, 1965

77. Morton Broffman (American, 1928–1992)

Students from Tuskegee Institute, Conclusion of the Selma to Montgomery March, Alabama, 1965

78. Morton Broffman (American, 1928–1992)

Conclusion of the Selma to Montgomery March, Alabama, 1965

79. Julian Wasser (American, born 1943)

Watts Riots, Los Angeles, California, 1965

80. Charles Brittin (American, born 1928)

CORE Demonstration against Employment Discrimination, Bogalusa, Louisiana, 1965

81. Jack Thornell (American, born 1940)

James Meredith Shot and Wounded During His March Against Fear,

Hernando, Mississippi, June 6, 1966

82. Jack Thornell (American, born 1940)

James Meredith Shot and Wounded During His March Against Fear,

Hernando, Mississippi, June 6, 1966

MPP060705-6/7/66-HERNANDO,MISS:James Meredith,with blood streaming from
his wounds,lies beside Mississippi highway 51 after he was shot from ambush
6/6.Police arrested Aubrey J.Norvell in the shooting and a preliminary hear-
ing will be held 6/7.   UPI TELEPHOTO

83. Sam Parrish (American, born 1941)

James Meredith Shot and Wounded During His March Against Fear,

Hernando, Mississippi, June 6, 1966

84. Unknown Photographer (United Press International)

Dr. Martin Luther King Jr., Floyd McKissick, and Stokely Carmichael March Arm in Arm,

Canton, Mississippi, July 1, 1966

85. Gordon Parks (American, 1912–2006)

Stokely Carmichael at a Meeting in Watts, California, 1966

86. Steve Schapiro (American, born 1936)

Dr. Martin Luther King's Motel Room After He Was Shot, Memphis, Tennessee, 1968

87. Constantine Manos (American, born 1934)

Coretta King and Family around the Open Casket at the Funeral of Dr. Martin Luther King Jr.,

Atlanta, Georgia, 1968

88. Bob Adelman (American, born 1930)

Dr. Martin Luther King Jr. Lying in State, Atlanta, Georgia, 1968

89. Bob Fitch (American, born 1939)

Dr. Martin Luther King Jr. Funeral with Mrs. King, Her Children, and Harry Belafonte,

Atlanta, Georgia, April 9, 1968

90. Donald Blumberg (American, born 1935)

Dr. Martin Luther King's Funeral, 1968

91. James E. Hinton (American, 1936–2006)

Man Beaten by Police, Night of Dr. King's Assassination, Harlem, New York, April 4, 1968

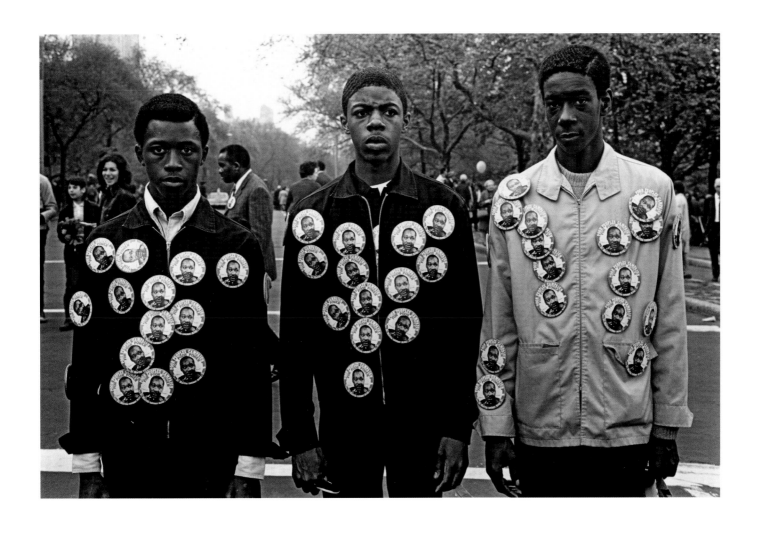

92. Benedict J. Fernandez (American, born 1936)

Memorial to Dr. Martin Luther King Jr., Central Park, New York City, April 5, 1968

93. Ernest C. Withers (American, 1922–2007)

Sanitation Workers Strike, Memphis, Tennessee, March 28, 1968

94. Builder Levy (American, born 1942)

I Am a Man / Union Justice Now, Martin Luther King Memorial March for Union Justice

and to End Racism, Memphis, Tennessee, 1968

95. Constantine Manos (American, born 1934)

Jesse Jackson Addresses the Crowd, Resurrection City, Poor People's Campaign,

Washington, D.C., 1968

96. LeRoy W. Henderson (American, born 1936)

Resurrection City, Poor People's Campaign, Washington, D.C., 1968

97. Morton Broffman (American, 1928–1992)

Poor People's Campaign, Washington, D.C., 1968

98. Larry Fink (American, born 1941)

Coretta Scott King, Poor People's Campaign, Washington, D.C., 1968

John Lewis

Afterword

These powerful images are not make-believe. They are real portraits of American history just the way it happened not too long ago in the Deep South. These pictures are an outgrowth of the struggles, the suffering, and the strains of humanity yearning to throw off the yoke of oppression. They are a testament to the ability of a committed, determined people to transform a nation, even the most powerful nation on earth, and bring it more in line with the call for justice.

If you could not join the sit-ins, the Freedom Rides, or the marches; if you were not born at a time when you could attend the nonviolence training or the community organizing meetings, then there is no better way for you to learn what the civil rights movement was all about than to look into the faces of humanity captured in these photographs.

It took nothing short of raw courage for participants in the movement to stand up to the governor, to the citizens' council, to mounted police, tear gas, fire hoses, and attack dogs. It was dangerous—very dangerous—for anyone to say no to segregation and racial discrimination simply by taking a seat at an integrated lunch counter or on a public bus. It was almost like committing suicide for an African American to go to the courthouse in the Delta of Mississippi or the Black Belt of Alabama and declare his or her intention to register to vote. White organizers were risking their lives trying to register black Americans to vote. The cameras of reporters, their pads and pens, were seen by segregationists as an invitation to brutality.

Our homes were bombed and our jobs were threatened. Some of us were expelled from college or run out of town. Peaceful, nonviolent protesters were trampled by horses, struck with bull whips, beaten with nightsticks, arrested, and taken to jail. Some were shot and even killed, but we buried our dead and kept on coming. We knew we would not stop; we would never turn back until we tore down the walls of legalized segregation.

We didn't have a cell phone. We didn't have a website. We didn't have a computer or even a fax machine, but we used what we had. We had ourselves, so we put our bodies on the line to make a difference in our society. We were just ordinary people with an extraordinary vision, imbued with the discipline and philosophy of nonviolence. We were convinced that if we adhered to the way of nonviolence as taught by Martin Luther King Jr. and Mahatma Gandhi, we could produce an all-inclusive world society—a Beloved Community—based on simple justice that values the dignity and the worth of every human being.

Central to our philosophic concept of the Beloved Community was an affirmation of faith in humanity—the willingness to believe that man has the moral capacity to care for his fellow man. When we suffered violence and abuse, our concern was not for retaliation. We sought to understand the human condition of our attackers and to accept the suffering in the right spirit. We believed that ends and means were inseparable, so if we wanted to create a peaceful society, then we had to use the methods of peace and goodwill. Our protests were love in action. We were attempting to redeem not only our attackers, but the very soul of America.

Perhaps the greatest and most timeless gift of this history is that it serves as a reminder that you can make a difference. No matter how fierce your adversary, no matter how organized the opposition, no matter how powerful the resistance, nothing can stop the movement of a disciplined, determined people. These images make it plain that we are standing on the shoulders of the martyrs of the civil rights movement.

We must never forget that men and women gave their lives for our democracy. Some of them are the martyrs we knew—Martin Luther King Jr., Andrew Goodman, Mickey Schwerner, James Chaney, Viola Liuzzo, Jimmie Lee Jackson—others are countless and nameless. But they gave their lives so that we might live in a better nation today. Through these photographs we can see their pain, their struggle, and their sacrifice. They have informed us with their testimony of faith, and they leave us with a legacy, a mission, and a mandate. We must do our part to make sure that these men, women, and children did not live and die in vain.

We are fortunate in our society that a means of resistance has been built into the law and the political process—the vote. The vote is the most powerful nonviolent tool we have in a democracy. We must use our votes, our power, and our organizational abilities to create a movement for good. We must not give up this power. We must not give in. We must not give out. We must use what we have—all of our talents, resources, energy, and creativity. We must do all we can to help build a better nation and a better world.

In the 1960s, this nation witnessed a nonviolent revolution under the rule of law, a revolution of values, a revolution of ideas. We have come a great distance in just a few decades, but we still have a distance to go before we build the Beloved Community. There is still a need to change the social, political, economic, and religious structures around us. There is still a need for a revolution of values and ideas in this nation and throughout the world. There is still a need to build a Beloved Community, a nation and a world at peace with itself.

List of Plates

1. Dan Weiner (American, 1919–1959)
Dr. Martin Luther King Jr. Addressing a Mass Meeting at First Baptist Church, Montgomery, Alabama, 1956
Gelatin silver print
8¹³⁄₁₆ × 13⅜ inches (22.4 × 34 cm)
High Museum of Art, 2007.256
Purchase with funds from Jess and Sherri Crawford in honor of John Lewis

2. Unknown Photographer (*New York Times*)
Rosa Parks Being Fingerprinted, Montgomery, Alabama, February 22, 1956
Gelatin silver print
8⅛ × 8⅛ inches (20.6 × 20.6 cm)
High Museum of Art, 2007.113
Purchase with funds from Sandra Anderson Baccus in loving memory of Lloyd T. Baccus, M.D.

3. Ernest C. Withers (American, 1922–2007)
First Desegregated Bus Ride, Montgomery, Alabama, 1956
Gelatin silver print
14½ × 18½ inches (36.8 × 47 cm)
High Museum of Art, 2002.24.2
Purchase

4. Charles Moore (American, born 1931)
Dr. Martin Luther King Jr. Arrested, Montgomery, Alabama, 1958
Gelatin silver print
9⅛ × 13½ inches (23.1 × 34.3 cm)
High Museum of Art, 1994.63
Purchase with funds from Lucinda W. Bunnen for the Bunnen Collection

5. Unknown Photographer (*New York Times*)
Elizabeth Eckford Entering Central High School, Little Rock, Arkansas, September 5, 1957
Gelatin silver print
9⅜ × 7¾ inches (23.8 × 19.7 cm)
High Museum of Art, 2007.108
Purchase with funds from Sandra Anderson Baccus in loving memory of Lloyd T. Baccus, M.D.

6. Will Counts (American, 1931–1995)
L. Alex Wilson, Reporter for the Tri-State Defender, *Memphis, Attacked by a Crowd, Central High School, Little Rock, Arkansas*, September 23, 1957
Gelatin silver print
7⅛ × 9 inches (18.1 × 22.9 cm)
High Museum of Art, 2007.66
Purchase with funds from Charlotte and Jim Dixon

7. Unknown Photographer (Associated Press)
John Lewis and Jim Zwerg Beaten, Montgomery, Alabama, May 20, 1961
Gelatin silver print
6¾ × 9 inches (17.1 × 22.9 cm)
High Museum of Art, 2007.74
Purchase with funds from Charlotte and Jim Dixon

8. Horace Cort (American, active 1940s–1970s)
Another Bus Cancelled, Birmingham, Alabama, May 20, 1961
Gelatin silver print
5⅜ × 9¼ inches (13.7 × 23.5 cm)
High Museum of Art, 2007.75
Purchase with funds from Charlotte and Jim Dixon

9. Unknown Photographer (Associated Press)
National Guardsman, Montgomery Bus Station, Alabama, May 22, 1961
Gelatin silver print
8½ × 6½ inches (21.6 × 16.5 cm)
High Museum of Art, 2007.76
Purchase with funds from Charlotte and Jim Dixon

10. Bob Adelman (American, born 1930)
CORE Freedom Ride Bus, Westminster, Maryland, 1963
Gelatin silver print
6⅜ × 9⅝ inches (16.2 × 24.4 cm)
High Museum of Art, 2007.184
Purchase with funds from the H. B. and Doris Massey Charitable Trust

11. Donald Blumberg (American, born 1935)
Bus Rider, Mobilization for Youth, March on Washington, D.C., 1963
Gelatin silver print
12¾ × 8½ inches (32.4 × 21.6 cm);
High Museum of Art, 146.2008
Purchase with funds from Wanda Hopkins

12. Unknown Photographer (United Press International)
Winston Henry Lockett and Alfred David Jones Jr., Wake County Jail, Raleigh, North Carolina, August 15, 1962
Gelatin silver print
6½ × 9⅜ inches (16.5 × 23.8 cm)
High Museum of Art, 2007.92
Purchase with funds from Sandra Anderson Baccus in loving memory of Lloyd T. Baccus, M.D.

13. Unknown Photographer (*New York Times*)
Members of SNCC Praying at Burned-out Church, Dawson, Georgia, September 9, 1962
Gelatin silver print
8⅛ × 7⅜ inches (20.6 × 18.7 cm)
High Museum of Art, 2007.106
Purchase with funds from Sandra Anderson Baccus in loving memory of Lloyd T. Baccus, M.D.

14. Consuelo Kanaga (American, 1894–1978)
Peace and Freedom Walkers, Albany, Georgia, 1962
Gelatin silver print
12¹¹⁄₁₆ × 10¹¹⁄₁₆ inches (32.2 × 27.1 cm);
Collection of Dr. Charles and Lucille Plotz

15. Danny Lyon (American, born 1942)
A Terminal in the Delta, Clarksdale, Mississippi, 1962
Gelatin silver print
6½ × 9½ inches (16.5 × 24.1 cm)
High Museum of Art, 2007.208
Purchase with funds from Jess and Sherri Crawford in memory of Paul Robeson

16. Bob Adelman (American, born 1930)
Ferry across the Mississippi River, near Plaquemine, Louisiana, 1964
Gelatin silver print
6¹¹⁄₁₆ × 10 inches (17 × 25.4 cm)
High Museum of Art, 2007.178
Purchase with funds from Dr. Henrie M. Treadwell

17. Steve Schapiro (American, born 1936)
"Segregation Forever," Fort Lauderdale, Florida, 1964
Gelatin silver print
8¹¹⁄₁₆ × 13 inches (22 × 33 cm)
High Museum of Art, 2007.233
Purchase with funds from the H. B. and Doris Massey Charitable Trust

18. Bruce Davidson (American, born 1933)
Ku Klux Klan Rally, Atlanta, Georgia, 1962
Gelatin silver print
6⁵⁄₁₆ × 9⁷⁄₁₆ inches (16 × 23.9 cm)
High Museum of Art, 2007.261
Purchase with funds from Jess and Sherri Crawford in honor of John Lewis

19. Danny Lyon (American, born 1942)
Atlanta, Georgia, 1963
Gelatin silver print
6¼ × 9³⁄₁₆ inches (15.9 × 23.4 cm)
High Museum of Art, 2007.206
Purchase with funds from Jess and Sherri Crawford in memory of Paul Robeson

20. Danny Lyon (American, born 1942)
SNCC Office Staff, Atlanta, Georgia, 1963
Gelatin silver print
6⁵⁄₁₆ × 9⁹⁄₁₆ inches (16 × 24.3 cm)
High Museum of Art, 2007.207
Purchase with funds from Jess and Sherri Crawford in memory of Paul Robeson

21. Horace Cort (American, active 1940s–1970s)
Man Spraying Deodorant over Heads of Sit-in Demonstrators at Woolworth's, Atlanta, Georgia, October 20, 1960
Gelatin silver print
7¾ × 9½ inches (19.7 × 24.1 cm)
High Museum of Art, 2007.110
Purchase with funds from Sandra Anderson Baccus in loving memory of Lloyd T. Baccus, M.D.

22. Unknown Photographer (*New York Times*)
Civil Rights Demonstrators and Ku Klux Klan Members Share the Same Sidewalk, Atlanta, Georgia, January 25, 1964
Gelatin silver print
8½ × 11⅞ inches (21.6 × 30.2 cm)
High Museum of Art, 2007.98
Purchase with funds from Sandra Anderson Baccus in loving memory of Lloyd T. Baccus, M.D.

23. Bob Adelman (American, born 1930)
Picketers Arrested behind Loveman's Department Store, Birmingham, Alabama, May 1963
Gelatin silver print
6¾ × 9¾ inches (17.2 × 24.7 cm)
High Museum of Art, 2007.181
Purchase with funds from the H. B. and Doris Massey Charitable Trust

24. Bruce Davidson (American, born 1933)
Arresting Demonstrators, Birmingham, Alabama, May 1963
Gelatin silver print
6⁵⁄₁₆ × 9½ inches (16.1 × 24.1 cm)
High Museum of Art, 1995.69
Gift of Howard Greenberg

25. Bill Hudson (American, active 1940s–1970s)
Police Dog Attack, Birmingham, Alabama, May 3, 1963
Gelatin silver print
5⅞ × 8½ inches (14.9 × 21.6 cm)
High Museum of Art, 2007.100
Purchase with funds from Sandra Anderson Baccus in loving memory of Lloyd T. Baccus, M.D.

26. Unknown Photographer (*New York Times*)
Electric Cattle Prod, June 21, 1963
Gelatin silver print
6½ × 8⅝ inches (16.5 × 21.9 cm)
High Museum of Art, 2007.101
Purchase with funds from Sandra Anderson Baccus in loving memory of Lloyd T. Baccus, M.D.

27. Unknown Photographer (Associated Press)
Firemen Hosing Demonstrators, Kelly Ingram Park, Birmingham, Alabama, May 3, 1963
Gelatin silver print
5¾ × 8½ inches (14.6 × 21.6 cm)
High Museum of Art, 2007.96
Purchase with funds from Sandra Anderson Baccus in loving memory of Lloyd T. Baccus, M.D.

28. Bob Adelman (American, born 1930)
Firemen Hosing Demonstrators, Kelly Ingram Park, Birmingham, Alabama, May 3, 1963
Gelatin silver print
6¹¹⁄₁₆ × 9¹⁵⁄₁₆ inches (17 × 25.2 cm)
High Museum of Art, 2007.185
Purchase with funds from the H. B. and Doris Massey Charitable Trust

29. Bruce Davidson (American, born 1933)
Kelly Ingram Park, Birmingham, Alabama, May 3, 1963
Gelatin silver print
5¹⁄₁₆ × 7⁷⁄₁₆ inches (12.8 × 18.9 cm)
High Museum of Art, 2007.262
Purchase with funds from Jess and Sherri Crawford in honor of John Lewis

30. Bruce Davidson (American, born 1933)
Kelly Ingram Park, Birmingham, Alabama, May 3, 1963
Gelatin silver print
5¹⁄₁₆ × 7⁷⁄₁₆ inches (12.8 × 18.9 cm)
High Museum of Art, 2007.263
Purchase with funds from Jess and Sherri Crawford in honor of John Lewis

31. Charles Moore (American, born 1931)
Kelly Ingram Park, Birmingham, Alabama, May 3, 1963
Gelatin silver print
13⁷⁄₁₆ × 9³⁄₁₆ inches (34.2 × 23.4 cm)
High Museum of Art, 2007.246
Purchase with funds from Jess and Sherri Crawford in honor of John Lewis

32. Charles Moore (American, born 1931)
Kelly Ingram Park, Birmingham, Alabama, May 3, 1963
Gelatin silver print
9¼ × 13½ inches (23.4 × 34.5 cm)
High Museum of Art, 2007.269
Purchase with funds from Sandra Anderson Baccus in loving memory of Lloyd T. Baccus, M.D.

33. Moneta Sleet, Jr. (American, 1926–1996)
Dr. Martin Luther King in the Midst, March on Washington, D.C., 1963
Gelatin silver print
11⅛ × 17³⁄₁₆ inches (28.3 × 43.7 cm)
St. Louis Art Museum, 397:1991
Gift of the Johnson Publishing Company

34. Danny Lyon (American, born 1942)
John Lewis, March on Washington, D.C., 1963
Gelatin silver print
6⁵⁄₁₆ × 9⁵⁄₁₆ inches (16 × 23.7 cm)
Collection of Sir Elton John

35. Builder Levy (American, born 1942)
March on Washington, D.C., 1963
Gelatin silver print
13⁷⁄₁₆ × 10½ inches (34.1 × 26.6 cm);
High Museum of Art, 2007.200
Purchase with funds from Dr. Henrie M. Treadwell

36. Declan Haun (American, 1937–1994)
Picketing the Courthouse, Monroe, North Carolina, August 26, 1961
Gelatin silver print
13⁷⁄₁₆ × 9 inches (34.2 × 22.9 cm)
High Museum of Art, 1994.64
Purchase with funds from the H. B. and Doris Massey Charitable Trust and Lucinda W. Bunnen for the Bunnen Collection

37. Declan Haun (American, 1937–1994)
Dr. Martin Luther King Jr. Arriving at the 16th Street Baptist Church, Birmingham, Alabama, 1963
Gelatin silver print
9⅝ × 6⅝ inches (24.5 × 16.9 cm)
High Museum of Art, 2006.35
Purchase with funds from the H. B. and Doris Massey Charitable Trust, Wanda and Lindsey Hopkins III, and Lucinda W. Bunnen for the Bunnen Collection

38. Declan Haun (American, 1937–1994)
16th Street Baptist Church, Birmingham, Alabama, 1963
Gelatin silver print
10¹⁵⁄₁₆ × 8¹⁵⁄₁₆ inches (27.8 × 22.7 cm)
High Museum of Art, 2006.47
Purchase with funds from the H. B. and Doris Massey Charitable Trust, Wanda and Lindsey Hopkins III, and Lucinda W. Bunnen for the Bunnen Collection

39. Danny Lyon (American, born 1942)
SNCC Photographer Clifford Vaughs is Arrested by the National Guard, Cambridge, Maryland, 1964
Gelatin silver print
9 × 14⁷⁄₁₆ inches (22.9 × 36.7 cm)
High Museum of Art, 2006.238.27
Gift of Turner Broadcasting System, Inc.

40. Danny Lyon (American, born 1942)
Stokely Carmichael, Confrontation with National Guard, Cambridge, Maryland, 1964
Gelatin silver print
6½ × 8¾ inches (16.5 × 22.2 cm)
High Museum of Art, 2007.214
Purchase with funds from Joan N. Whitcomb

41. Steve Schapiro (American, born 1936)
The Civil Rights Workers' Station Wagon, Philadelphia, Mississippi, 1964
Gelatin silver print
8¹¹⁄₁₆ × 13 inches (22 × 33 cm)
High Museum of Art, 2007.222
Purchase with funds from the H. B. and Doris Massey Charitable Trust

42. Bill Eppridge (American, born 1938)
Chaney Family as They Depart for the Funeral of James Chaney, Philadelphia, Mississippi, 1964
Gelatin silver print
8⁵⁄₁₆ × 12⁵⁄₁₆ inches (21.1 × 31.3 cm)
High Museum of Art, 2007.194
Purchase with funds from Jeff and Valerie Levy

43. Declan Haun (American, 1937–1994)
Voting Booth, Alabama, 1965
Gelatin silver print
8⅞ × 13¹⁄₁₆ inches (22.6 × 33.1 cm)
High Museum of Art, 2006.48
Purchase with funds from the H. B. and Doris Massey Charitable Trust, Wanda and Lindsey Hopkins III, and Lucinda W. Bunnen for the Bunnen Collection

44. Bob Adelman (American, born 1930)
Box in Frank Robinson's CORE Voter Registration Office, Sumter, South Carolina, 1962
Gelatin silver print
7³⁄₁₆ × 10½ inches (18.2 × 26.7 cm)
High Museum of Art, 2007.176
Purchase with funds from the H. B. and Doris Massey Charitable Trust

45. Bob Adelman (American, born 1930)
Prospective Voter Studies Sample Voter Registration Form in CORE Office, Sumter, South Carolina, 1962
Gelatin silver print
6½ × 9⁹⁄₁₆ inches (16.5 × 24.3 cm)
High Museum of Art, 2007.180
Purchase with funds from Earnest and Charlene Crusoe-Ingram

46. Bob Adelman (American, born 1930)
Woman Registering to Vote, Sumter, South Carolina, 1962
Gelatin silver print
6¹³⁄₁₆ × 10³⁄₁₆ inches (17.3 × 25.8 cm)
High Museum of Art, 2007.183
Purchase with funds from the H. B. and Doris Massey Charitable Trust

47. James Kerlin (American, active 1940s–1970s)
Cleaning the Pool, St. Augustine, Florida, June 18, 1964
Gelatin silver print
8⅜ × 6⅞ inches (21.3 × 17.5 cm)
High Museum of Art, 2006.84
Purchase

48. Unknown Photographer
Dr. Martin Luther King Jr. and Rev. Ralph Abernathy, John's County Jail, St. Augustine, Florida, 1964
Gelatin silver print
8½ × 6½ inches (21.8 × 16.6 cm)
High Museum of Art, 147.2008
Purchase with funds from Dr. Elaine Levin

49. Declan Haun (American, 1937–1994)
Man Praying, Selma, Alabama, 1965
Gelatin silver print
13⁷⁄₁₆ × 9⅛ inches (34.2 × 23.2 cm)
High Museum of Art, 2006.46
Purchase with funds from the H. B. and Doris Massey Charitable Trust, Wanda and Lindsey Hopkins III, and Lucinda W. Bunnen for the Bunnen Collection

50. Bob Adelman (American, born 1930)
Woman Being Arrested, Downstate Medical Center, Brooklyn, New York, 1963
Gelatin silver print
6½ × 9¹³⁄₁₆ inches (16.5 × 24.9 cm)
High Museum of Art, 2007.173
Gift of the artist

51. Bob Adelman (American, born 1930)
Dr. Martin Luther King Jr., Camden, Alabama, 1966
Gelatin silver print
9¹⁄₁₆ × 9¹⁄₁₆ inches (23 × 23 cm)
High Museum of Art, 2007.240
Purchase with funds from Jess and Sherri Crawford in honor of John Lewis

52. Marvin Roth (American, active 1940s–1970s)
Fannie Lou Hamer, ca. 1964
Gelatin silver print
7¹¹⁄₁₆ × 7¹³⁄₁₆ inches (19.5 × 19.8 cm)
High Museum of Art, 2007.255
Purchase with funds from Jess and Sherri Crawford in honor of John Lewis

53. Steve Schapiro (American, born 1936)
Fannie Lou Hamer at Home, Ruleville, Mississippi, 1963
Gelatin silver print
13 × 8¹¹⁄₁₆ inches (33 × 22 cm)
High Museum of Art, 2007.227
Purchase with funds from the H. B. and Doris Massey Charitable Trust

54. Bob Fitch (American, born 1939)
Dr. Martin Luther King Jr. in the SCLC Office, Atlanta, Georgia, 1966
Gelatin silver print
12¹⁵⁄₁₆ × 8⅞ inches (32.8 × 22.6 cm)
High Museum of Art, 2007.68
Purchase with funds from Charlotte and Jim Dixon

55. Gordon Parks (American, 1912–2006)
Muslim Boy Selling Newspapers, 1963
Gelatin silver print
8¹¹⁄₁₆ × 12¹⁵⁄₁₆ inches (22.1 × 32.9 cm)
Courtesy Howard Greenberg Gallery

56. Leonard Freed (American, 1929–2006)
CORE Demonstration, Brooklyn, New York, 1963
Gelatin silver print
13⅝ × 10¹⁄₁₆ inches (34.6 × 25.5 cm)
High Museum of Art, 2005.309
Purchase

57. Doris Derby (American, born 1939)
L. C. Dorsey, Civil Rights Worker from Shelby,
Mississippi, at the Vegetable Cooperative,
Ruleville, Mississippi, 1968
Gelatin silver print
14 × 9½ inches (35.5 × 24.2 cm)
High Museum of Art, 2007.190
Purchase with funds from Jeff and Valerie Levy

58. Doris Derby (American, born 1939)
Nurse and Doctor, Health Clinic in the Mississippi
Delta, 1968
Gelatin silver print
14 × 9½ inches (35.5 × 24.2 cm)
High Museum of Art, 2007.189
Purchase with funds from Jeff and Valerie Levy

59. Unknown Photographer (*New York Times*)
Protestors against Dallas County Sheriff Jim Clark
and Segregation, Selma, Alabama, 1965
Gelatin silver print
6¾ × 8⅝ inches (17.1 × 21.9 cm)
High Museum of Art, 2007.103
Purchase with funds from Sandra Anderson Baccus
in loving memory of Lloyd T. Baccus, M.D.

60. Declan Haun (American, 1937–1994)
Caricature of Sheriff Jim Clark and a Drawing of
Dr. Martin Luther King Jr. Posted on a Wall, Selma,
Alabama, 1965
Gelatin silver print
9½ × 6⅝₁₆ inches (24.2 × 16.1 cm)
High Museum of Art, 2006.40
Purchase with funds from the H. B. and Doris Massey
Charitable Trust, Wanda and Lindsey Hopkins III,
and Lucinda W. Bunnen for the Bunnen Collection

61. James "Spider" Martin (American, 1939–2003)
State Trooper Gives Marchers "Two Minute
Warning," Selma, Alabama, March 7, 1965
Gelatin silver print
6 × 9¹⁄₁₆ inches (15.2 × 23 cm)
High Museum of Art, 2007.215
Purchase with funds from Kristie and Charles Abney

62. James "Spider" Martin (American, 1939–2003)
Amelia Boynton Beaten by State Troopers,
Selma, Alabama, March 7, 1965
Gelatin silver print
9 × 6 inches (22.8 × 15.3 cm)
High Museum of Art, 2007.216
Purchase with funds from Kristie and Charles Abney

63. Unknown Photographer
State Troopers Break Up Marchers,
Selma, Alabama, March 7, 1965
Gelatin silver print
6¾ × 8⅝ inches (17.1 × 21.9 cm)
High Museum of Art, 2007.102
Purchase with funds from Sandra Anderson Baccus
in loving memory of Lloyd T. Baccus, M.D.

64. Steve Schapiro (American, born 1936)
Andrew Young, Martin Luther King Jr., and
John Lewis, Selma, Alabama, 1965
Gelatin silver print
13 × 8¹¹⁄₁₆ inches (33 × 22 cm)
High Museum of Art, 2007.219
Purchase with funds from the H. B. and
Doris Massey Charitable Trust

65. Charles Moore (American, born 1931)
Freedom Singing, Selma, Alabama, 1965
Gelatin silver print
7⅝ × 11⅛ inches (19.4 × 28.3 cm)
High Museum of Art, 2007.252
Purchase with funds from Jess and Sherri Crawford
in honor of John Lewis

66. Matt Herron (American, born 1931)
James Baldwin, Joan Baez, and James Forman,
Selma to Montgomery March, Alabama, 1965
Gelatin silver print
6⅝ × 9¹³⁄₁₆ inches (16.9 × 24.9 cm)
High Museum of Art, 2007.239
Purchase with funds from Jess and Sherri Crawford
in honor of John Lewis

67. Matt Herron (American, born 1931)
Selma to Montgomery March, Alabama, 1965
Gelatin silver print
5¼ × 9¹¹⁄₁₆ inches (13.3 × 24.6 cm)
High Museum of Art, 2007.244
Purchase with funds from Jess and Sherri Crawford
in honor of John Lewis

68. Moneta Sleet, Jr. (American, 1926–1996)
Marchers on the Road to Montgomery, Alabama,
1965
Gelatin silver print
13¼ × 19¾ inches (33.7 × 50.2 cm)
St. Louis Art Museum, 413:1991
Gift of the Johnson Publishing Company

69. James H. Karales (American, 1930–2002)
Bystanders, Selma to Montgomery March, Alabama,
1965
Gelatin silver print
5⅞ × 8¾ inches (14.9 × 22.5 cm)
High Museum of Art, 2007.270
Purchase with funds from Sandra Anderson Baccus
in loving memory of Lloyd T. Baccus, M.D.

70. Declan Haun (American, 1937–1994)
Children in the Crowd, Selma, Alabama, 1965
Gelatin silver print
5⅞ × 8⁹⁄₁₆ inches (14.9 × 21.7 cm)
High Museum of Art, 2006.49
Purchase with funds from the H.B. and Doris Massey
Charitable Trust, Wanda and Lindsey Hopkins III,
and Lucinda W. Bunnen for the Bunnen Collection

71. Ivan Massar (American, born 1924)
*Dr. Martin Luther King Jr., Coretta Scott King,
John Lewis, and Others, Selma to Montgomery
March, Alabama*, 1965
Gelatin silver print
6¹¹⁄₁₆ × 10¾ inches (17 × 27.3 cm)
High Museum of Art, 2007.72
Purchase with funds from Charlotte and Jim Dixon

72. Moneta Sleet, Jr. (American, (1926–1996)
*Dr. King and Coretta Scott King Singing in the Rain,
Selma to Montgomery March, Alabama*, 1965
Gelatin silver print
19¾ × 13⅜ inches (50.2 × 34 cm)
St. Louis Art Museum, 395:1991
Gift of the Johnson Publishing Company

73. Steve Schapiro (American, born 1936)
*Boy with American Flag, Selma to Montgomery
March, Alabama*, 1965
Gelatin silver print
8¹¹⁄₁₆ × 13 inches (22 × 33 cm)
High Museum of Art, 2007.230
Purchase with funds from the H.B. and Doris Massey
Charitable Trust

74. Morton Broffman (American, 1928–1992)
*Conclusion of the Selma to Montgomery March,
Alabama*, 1965
Gelatin silver print
9⅝ × 6⁹⁄₁₆ inches (24.5 × 16.6 cm)
High Museum of Art, 2007.65
Gift of the Broffman Family

75. Steve Schapiro (American, born 1936)
*Andrew Young, Rev. Ralph Abernathy, and
Dr. Martin Luther King Jr., Selma to Montgomery
March, Alabama*, 1965
Gelatin silver print
8¹¹⁄₁₆ × 13 inches (22 × 33 cm)
High Museum of Art, 2007.223
Purchase with funds from the H.B. and Doris Massey
Charitable Trust

76. Morton Broffman (American, 1928–1992)
*Dr. King and Coretta Scott King Leading Marchers,
Montgomery, Alabama*, 1965
Gelatin silver print
5⁷⁄₁₆ × 7¹³⁄₁₆ inches (13.8 × 19.9 cm)
High Museum of Art, 2007.34
Gift of the Broffman Family

77. Morton Broffman (American, 1928–1992)
*Students from Tuskegee Institute, Conclusion of
the Selma to Montgomery March, Alabama*, 1965
Gelatin silver print
5⅞ × 7¹⁵⁄₁₆ inches (14.9 × 20.2 cm)
High Museum of Art, 2007.46
Gift of the Broffman Family

78. Morton Broffman (American, 1928–1992)
*Conclusion of the Selma to Montgomery March,
Alabama*, 1965
Gelatin silver print
7⅜ × 9¹⁄₁₆ inches (18.8 × 23 cm)
High Museum of Art, 2007.49
Gift of the Broffman Family

79. Julian Wasser (American, born 1943)
Watts Riots, Los Angeles, California, 1965
Gelatin silver print
10 × 13⁵⁄₁₆ inches (25.4 × 33.8 cm)
High Museum of Art, 2007.273
Purchase

80. Charles Brittin (American, born 1928)
*CORE Demonstration against Employment
Discrimination, Bogalusa, Louisiana*, 1965
Gelatin silver print
9¼ × 13⁹⁄₁₆ inches (23.5 × 34.4 cm)
High Museum of Art, 2007.257
Purchase with funds from Jess and Sherri Crawford
in honor of John Lewis

81. Jack Thornell (American, born 1940)
James Meredith Shot and Wounded During
His March Against Fear, Hernando, Mississippi,
June 6, 1966
Gelatin silver print
6⅜ × 10⅜ inches (16.2 × 26.4 cm)
Collection of Dan and Mary Solomon

82. Jack Thornell (American, born 1940)
James Meredith Shot and Wounded During
His March Against Fear, Hernando, Mississippi,
June 6, 1966
Gelatin silver print
6⅝ × 8⅜ inches (16.8 × 21.3 cm)
Collection of Dan and Mary Solomon

83. Sam Parrish (American, born 1941)
James Meredith Shot and Wounded During
His March Against Fear, Hernando, Mississippi,
June 6, 1966
Gelatin silver print
6⅞ × 9½ inches (17.5 × 24.1 cm)
High Museum of Art, 2007.105
Purchase with funds from Sandra Anderson Baccus
in loving memory of Lloyd T. Baccus, M.D.

84. Unknown Photographer (United Press
International)
Dr. Martin Luther King Jr., Floyd McKissick,
and Stokely Carmichael March Arm in Arm,
Canton, Mississippi, July 1, 1966
Gelatin silver print
6½ × 9⅜ inches (16.5 × 23.8 cm)
High Museum of Art, 2007.94
Purchase with funds from Sandra Anderson Baccus
in loving memory of Lloyd T. Baccus, M.D.

85. Gordon Parks (American, 1912–2006)
Stokely Carmichael at a Meeting in Watts,
California, 1966
Gelatin silver print
10 × 13⁷⁄₁₆ inches (25.4 × 34.1 cm)
Courtesy Howard Greenberg Gallery

86. Steve Schapiro (American, born 1936)
Dr. Martin Luther King's Motel Room After
He Was Shot, Memphis, Tennessee, 1968
Gelatin silver print
8¹¹⁄₁₆ × 13 inches (22 × 33 cm)
High Museum of Art, 2007.225
Purchase with funds from the H. B. and
Doris Massey Charitable Trust

87. Constantine Manos (American, born 1934)
Coretta King and Family around the Open Casket
at the Funeral of Dr. Martin Luther King Jr., Atlanta,
Georgia, 1968
Gelatin silver print
6¹⁄₁₆ × 9 inches (15.4 × 22.8 cm)
High Museum of Art, 2006.164
Gift of the artist

88. Bob Adelman (American, born 1930)
Dr. Martin Luther King Jr. Lying in State,
Atlanta, Georgia, 1968
Gelatin silver print
6½ × 9½ inches (16.5 × 24.2 cm)
High Museum of Art, 2007.174
Gift of the artist

89. Bob Fitch (American, born 1939)
Dr. Martin Luther King Jr. Funeral with
Mrs. King, Her Children, and Harry Belafonte,
Atlanta, Georgia, April 9, 1968
Gelatin silver print
6¾ × 9½ inches (17.1 × 24.1 cm)
High Museum of Art, 2007.67
Purchase with funds from Charlotte and Jim Dixon

90. Donald Blumberg (American, born 1935)
Dr. Martin Luther King's Funeral, 1968
Gelatin silver print
16 × 20 inches (40 × 50 cm)
High Museum of Art, 2007.186
Purchase

91. James E. Hinton (American, 1936–2006)
Man Beaten by Police, Night of Dr. King's
Assassination, Harlem, New York, April 4, 1968
Gelatin silver print
13 × 19 inches (33 × 48.3 cm)
High Museum of Art, 2001.100
Purchase with funds from Jan P. and Warren J.
Adelson

92. Benedict J. Fernandez (American, born 1936)
Memorial to Dr. Martin Luther King Jr.,
Central Park, New York City, April 5, 1968
Gelatin silver print
8⅛ × 13 inches (20.7 × 33 cm)
High Museum of Art, 1999.154.7
Gift of Gloria and Paul Sternberg

93. Ernest C. Withers (American, 1922–2007)
Sanitation Workers Strike, Memphis, Tennessee,
March 28, 1968
Gelatin silver print
10½ × 18½ inches (26.7 × 47 cm)
High Museum of Art, 2002.24.1
Purchase

94. Builder Levy (American, born 1942)
I Am a Man / Union Justice Now, Martin Luther
King Memorial March for Union Justice and to End
Racism, Memphis, Tennessee, 1968
Gelatin silver print
7½ × 11 inches (19.1 × 27.9 cm)
High Museum of Art, 2007.199
Purchase with funds from the H. B. and Doris Massey
Charitable Trust

95. Constantine Manos (American, born 1934)
Jesse Jackson Addresses the Crowd, Resurrection
City, Poor People's Campaign, Washington, D.C.,
1968
Gelatin silver print
6⅜ × 9⅜ inches (16.2 × 23.8 cm)
High Museum of Art, 2006.167
Gift of the artist

96. LeRoy W. Henderson (American, born 1936)
Resurrection City, Poor People's Campaign,
Washington, D.C., 1968
Gelatin silver print
11 × 14 inches (27.9 × 35.6 cm)
Collection of the artist

97. Morton Broffman (American, 1928–1992)
Poor People's Campaign, Washington, D.C., 1968
Gelatin silver print
10¹³⁄₁₆ × 13¾ inches (27.5 × 35 cm)
High Museum of Art, 2007.36
Gift of the Broffman Family

98. Larry Fink (American, born 1941)
Coretta Scott King, Poor People's Campaign,
Washington, D.C., 1968
Gelatin silver print
12¹¹⁄₁₆ × 8⅝ inches (32.2 × 21.9 cm)
High Museum of Art, 2007.196
Purchase with funds provided by Earnest and
Charlene Crusoe-Ingram

Selected Bibliography

Albert, Peter J., and Ronald Hoffman, eds. *We Shall Overcome*. New York: Da Capo Press, 1990. 14, no. 2 (May 1976): 12–14.

Allen, Ivan Jr., and Paul Hemphill. *Mayor: Notes on the Sixties*. New York: Simon and Schuster, 1971.

Anderson, Jervis. *Bayard Rustin: Troubles I've Seen: A Biography*. New York: HarperCollins, 1997.

Arsenault, Raymond. *Freedom Riders: 1961 and the Struggle for Racial Justice*. New York: Oxford University Press, 2006.

Ashmore, Harry S. *Civil Rights and Wrongs: A Memoir of Race and Politics, 1944–1996*. Columbia: University of South Carolina Press, 1997.

Associated Press and David Halberstam. *Breaking News: How the Associated Press Has Covered War, Peace, and Everything Else*. New York: Princeton Architectural Press, 2007.

Bailey, Ronald W., and Michèle Furst, eds. *Let Us March On! Selected Civil Rights Photographs of Ernest C. Withers, 1955–1968*. Boston: Massachusetts College of Art, 1992.

Beals, Melba Patillo. *Warriors Don't Cry: A Searing Memoir of the Battle to Integrate Little Rock's Central High*. New York: Washington Square Press, 1994.

Belfrage, Sally. *Freedom Summer*. Charlottesville and London: University Press of Virginia, 1990.

Blumberg, Rhoda Lois. *Civil Rights: The 1960s Freedom Struggle*. Boston: Twayne Publishers, 1984.

Booker, Simeon. *Black Man's America*. Englewood Cliffs, N.J.: Prentice-Hall, 1964.

Branch, Taylor. *Parting the Waters: America in the King Years, 1954–63*. New York: Simon & Schuster, 1988.

———. *Pillar of Fire: America in the King Years, 1963–65*. New York: Simon and Schuster, 1998.

———. *At Canaan's Edge: America in the King Years, 1965–68*. New York: Simon & Schuster, 2006.

Brinkley, Douglas. *Rosa Parks*. New York: Viking, 2000.

Bullard, Sara, ed. *Free at Last: A History of the Civil Rights Movement and Those Who Died in the Struggle*. Montgomery, Ala.: Southern Poverty Law Center, 1989.

Cagin, Seth, and Philip Dray. *We Are Not Afraid: The Story of Goodman, Schwerner, and Chaney and the Civil Rights Campaign for Mississippi*. New York: Macmillan, 1998.

Carawan, Guy, and Candie Carawan. *Sing for Freedom: The Story of the Civil Rights Movement Through Its Songs*. Bethlehem, Penn.: Sing Out Publications, 1990.

Carson, Clayborne. *In Struggle: SNCC and the Black Awakening of the 1960s*. Cambridge, Mass.: Harvard University Press, 1981.

Carson, Clayborne, David J. Garrow, Vincent Harding, and Darlene Clark Hine, eds. *Eyes on the Prize: A Reader and Guide*. New York: Penguin Books, 1987.

Chapnick, Howard. *Truth Needs No Ally: Inside Photojournalism*. Columbia: University of Missouri Press, 1994.

Chappell, David L. *Inside Agitators: White Southerners in the Civil Rights Movement*. Baltimore: Johns Hopkins University Press, 1994.

Cook, James Graham. *The Segregationists*. New York: Appleton-Century-Crofts, 1962.

Counts, Will, Will Campbell, Ernest Dumas, and Robert S. McCord. *A Life Is More Than a Moment: The Desegregation of Little Rock's Central High*. Bloomington: Indiana University Press, 1999.

Crawford, Vicki L., Jacqueline Anne Rouse, and Barbara Woods, eds. *Women in the Civil Rights Movement: Trailblazers and Torchbearers, 1941–1965*. Bloomington and Indianapolis: Indiana University Press, 1993.

Davidson, Bruce. *Time of Change: Civil Rights Photographs, 1961–1965*. Los Angeles: St. Ann's Press, 2002.

Dittmer, John. *Local People: The Struggle for Civil Rights in Mississippi*. Urbana and Chicago: University of Illinois Press, 1994.

Eskew, Glenn T. *But for Birmingham: The Local and National Movements in the Civil Rights Struggle*. Chapel Hill: University of North Carolina Press, 1997.

Evans, Sara. *Personal Politics: The Roots of the Women's Liberation Movement in the Civil Rights Movement and the New Left*. New York: Knopf, 1979.

Fager, Charles E. *Selma: The March That Changed the South*. Boston: Beacon Press, 1985.

Fairclough, Adam. *To Redeem the Soul of America: The Southern Christian Leadership Conference and Martin Luther King Jr.* Athens: University of Georgia Press, 1987.

Galphin, Bruce. *The Riddle of Lester Maddox: An Unauthorized Biography*. Atlanta: Camelot Publishing, 1968.

Garrow, David J. *Protest at Selma: Martin Luther King and the Voting Rights Act of 1965*. New Haven, Conn., and London: Yale University Press, 1978.

———. *The FBI and Martin Luther King Jr.* New York: Penguin Books, 1981.

———. *Bearing the Cross: Martin Luther King Jr., and the Southern Christian Leadership Conference*. New York: Vintage Books, 1988.

Gitlin, Todd. *The Sixties: Years of Hope, Days of Rage*. New York: Bantam, 1989.

Halberstam, David. *The Children*. New York: Random House, 1998.

Hampton, Henry, and Steven Fayer. *Voices of Freedom: An Oral History of the Civil Rights Movement from the 1950s Through the 1980s*. New York: Bantam Books, 1991.

Hansberry, Lorraine. *The Movement: Documentary of a Struggle for Equality*. New York: Simon & Schuster, 1964.

Harding, Vincent. *Hope and History: Why We Must Share the History of the Movement*. Maryknoll, N.Y.: Orbis Books, 1990.

Hunter-Gault, Charlayne. *In My Place*. New York: Farrar Straus Giroux, 1992.

Kasher, Steven. *The Civil Rights Movement: A Photographic History, 1954–68*. New York: Abbeville Press, 1996.

King Jr., Martin Luther. *Stride Toward Freedom: The Montgomery Story*. New York: Harper and Brothers, 1958.

———. *Why We Can't Wait*. New York: New American Library, 1964.

———. *A Testament of Hope: The Essential Writings of Martin Luther King Jr.* Edited by James Melvin Washington. New York: HarperCollins Publishers, 1991.

King, Mary. *Freedom Song: A Personal Story of the 1960s Civil Rights Movement*. New York: William Morrow, 1987.

Kotz, Nick. *Judgment Days: Lyndon Baines Johnson, Martin Luther King Jr., and the Laws That Changed America*. Boston: Houghton Mifflin, 2005.

Levine, Ellen, ed. *Freedom's Children: Young Civil Rights Activists Tell Their Own Story*. New York: Avon Books, 1994.

Levy, Peter B. *Documentary History of the Modern Civil Rights Movement*. New York: Greenwood Press, 1992.

Lewis, Anthony. *Portrait of a Decade: The Second American Revolution*. New York: Random House, 1964.

Lewis, John, and Michael D'Orso. *Walking with the Wind: A Memoir of the Movement*. New York: Simon & Schuster, 1998.

Logue, Calvin M. *Ralph McGill: Editor and Publisher*. Durham, N.C.: Moore Publishing, 1969.

Long, Worth, Linn Shapiro, and Bernice Johnson Reagan. *We'll Never Turn Back*. Exhibition catalogue. Washington, D.C.: Smithsonian Performing Arts, 1980.

Lyon, Danny. *Memories of the Southern Civil Rights Movement*. Chapel Hill: University of North Carolina Press, 1992.

Marable, Manning. *Race, Reform, and Rebellion: The Second Reconstruction in Black America from 1945 to 1982*. Jackson: University Press of Mississippi, 1984.

McAdam, Doug. *Freedom Summer*. New York: Oxford University Press, 1988.

McGill, Ralph. *The South and the Southerner.* Boston: Little, Brown, 1963.

McWhorter, Diane. *Carry Me Home: Birmingham, Alabama, the Climactic Battle of the Civil Rights Revolution.* New York: Simon & Schuster, 2001.

Meier, August, and Elliot Rudwick. *CORE: A Study in the Civil Rights Movement, 1942–1968.* Urbana: University of Illinois Press, 1975.

Meier, August, John Bracey Jr., and Elliot Rudwick, eds. *Black Protest in the Sixties.* New York: Markus Wiener Publishing, 1991.

Meredith, James. *Three Years in Mississippi.* Bloomington: Indiana University Press, 1966.

Mills, Kay. *This Little Light of Mine: The Life of Fannie Lou Hamer.* New York: Dutton, 1993.

Moody, Anne. *Coming of Age in Mississippi.* New York: Dell, 1968.

Moore, Charles, and Michael Durham. *Powerful Days: The Civil Rights Photography of Charles Moore.* New York: Stewart, Tabori & Chang, 1991.

Morris, Aldon D. *The Origins of the Civil Rights Movement: Black Communities Organizing for Change.* New York: Free Press, 1984.

Murray, Paul T. *The Civil Rights Movement: References and Resources.* New York: G. K. Hall, 1993.

Myrdal, Gunnar, Richard Sterner, and Arnold Rose. *An American Dilemma.* New York: Harper & Brothers, 1944.

Nelson, Jack, and Jack Bass. *The Orangeburg Massacre.* New York: World Publishing, 1970.

Oppenheimer, Martin. *The Sit-in Movement of 1960.* Brooklyn: Carlson Publishing, 1989.

Peck, James. *Freedom Ride.* New York: Simon & Schuster, 1962.

Powledge, Fred. *Free at Last? The Civil Rights Movement and the People Who Made It.* Boston: Little, Brown, 1991.

Raines, Howell. *My Soul Is Rested.* New York: Penguin Books, 1983.

Randall, Herbert, and Bobs M. Tusa. *Faces of Freedom Summer.* Tuscaloosa and London: University of Alabama Press, 2001.

Roberts, Gene, and Hank Klibanoff. *The Race Beat: The Press, the Civil Rights Struggle, and the Awakening of a Nation.* New York: Alfred A. Knopf, 2006.

Robinson, Jo Ann Gibson. *The Montgomery Bus Boycott and the Women Who Started It.* Knoxville: University of Tennessee Press, 1987.

Romano, Renee C., and Leigh Raiford, eds. *The Civil Rights Movement in American Memory.* Athens and London: University of Georgia Press, 2006.

Rowe, Gary Thomas. *My Undercover Years with the Ku Klux Klan.* New York: Bantam Books, 1976.

Schulke, Flip. *He Had a Dream: Martin Luther King Jr. and the Civil Rights Movement.* New York: W. W. Norton, 1995.

———. *Martin Luther King Jr.: A Documentary, Montgomery to Memphis.* New York: Norton, 1976.

Seeger, Pete, and Bob Reiser. *Everybody Says Freedom.* New York: W. W. Norton, 1989.

Sitkoff, Howard. *The Struggle for Black Equality, 1954–1980.* New York: Hill and Wang, 1981.

Sokol, Jason. *There Goes My Everything: White Southerners in the Age of Civil Rights, 1945–1975.* New York: Alfred A. Knopf, 2006.

Weisbrot, Robert. *Freedom Bound: A History of America's Civil Rights Movement.* New York: Plume, 1991.

West, Cornel. *Race Matters.* Boston: Beacon Press, 1993.

Whitfield, Stephen J. *A Death in the Delta: The Story of Emmett Till.* New York: Free Press, 1988.

Williams, Juan. *Eyes on the Prize: America's Civil Rights Years, 1954–65.* New York: Viking Press, 1987.

Withers, Ernest C. *I Am a Man: Photographs of the 1969 Memphis Sanitation Strike and Dr. Martin Luther King Jr.* Memphis: Memphis Publishing, 1993.

———. *Let Us March On! Selected Civil Rights Photographs of Ernest C. Withers, 1955–1968.* Boston: Massachusetts College of Art and Northeastern University, 1992.

Young, Andrew. *An Easy Burden: The Civil Rights Movement and the Transformation of America.* New York: HarperCollins, 1996.

Zinn, Howard. *SNCC: The New Abolitionists.* Boston: Beacon Press, 1964.

Photography Credits

All images photographed by Peter Harholdt except pl. 18, figs. 16 and 22, and pls. 33, 68, 72, and 96.

Frontispiece; fig. 2 (p. 16); pl. 69: © James H. Karales, courtesy Estate of James Karales

Title page: © Dennis Brack

Figs. 1 (p. 15), 9; pls. 15, 19, 20, 34, 39, 40: © Danny Lyon/Magnum Photos, courtesy Edwynn Houk Gallery

Figs. 1 (p. 20), 12, 17, 18: © Lonnie J. Wilson, courtesy of Vicki Wilson Hunt

Fig. 2 (p. 22); pls. 33, 68, 72: © Johnson Publishing Company

Fig. 3 (p. 17); pls. 7, 9: Associated Press/Wide World Photos

Fig. 3 (p. 23); pls. 61, 62: © James "Spider" Martin, courtesy Spider Martin Civil Rights Collection

Figs. 4, 21; pls. 74, 76–78, 97: © Morton Broffman, courtesy of the Broffman family

Figs. 5, 6; pls. 8, 21: © Horace Cort and Associated Press/Wide World Photos

Fig. 7: © Joseph Postiglione and United Press International/Corbis-Bettmann

Fig. 8: © Bob Fletcher, courtesy of the photographer

Fig. 10: © George Cook, courtesy of the photographer

Fig. 11; pl. 42: © Bill Eppridge, courtesy of the photographer

Fig. 13; pls. 10, 16, 23, 28, 44–46, 50, 51, 88; cover: © Bob Adelman/Magnum Photos

Fig. 14; pls. 4, 31, 32, 65: © Charles Moore/Black Star, courtesy Howard Greenberg Gallery

Fig. 15; pl. 25: © Bill Hudson and Associated Press/Wide World Photos

Fig. 16; pls. 2, 5, 13, 22, 59: © *New York Times*

Fig. 19; pls. 18, 24, 29, 30: © Bruce Davidson/Magnum Photos

Fig. 20; pls. 57, 58: © Doris Derby, courtesy of the photographer

Fig. 22; pls. 26, 27, 48, 63: Unknown Photographers

Pl. 1: © Dan Weiner, courtesy Sandra Weiner

Pls. 3, 93: © Ernest C. Withers, courtesy Panopticon Gallery

Pl. 6: © Will Counts and Associated Press/Wide World Photos

Pls. 11, 19: © Donald Blumberg, courtesy of the photographer

Pls. 12, 84: United Press International/Corbis-Bettmann

Pl. 14: © Consuelo Kanaga

Pls. 17, 41, 53, 64, 73, 75, 86: © Steve Schapiro/Black Star

Pls. 35, 94: © Builder Levy, courtesy of the photographer

Pls. 36–38, 43, 49, 60, 70, 90: © Declan Haun/Black Star

Pl. 47: © James Kerlin and Associated Press/Wide World Photos

Pl. 52: © Marvin Roth, courtesy Howard Greenberg Gallery

Pls. 54, 89: © Bob Fitch/Black Star, courtesy of the photographer

Pls. 55, 85: © Gordon Parks, courtesy Howard Greenberg Gallery

Pl. 56: © Leonard Freed/Magnum Photos

Pls. 66, 67: © Matt Herron/Take Stock, courtesy Howard Greenberg Gallery

Pl. 71; back cover: © Ivan Massar/Black Star

Pl. 79: © Julian Wasser, courtesy Craig Krull Gallery

Pl. 80: © Charles Brittin, courtesy of the photographer

Pls. 81, 82: © Jack Thornell and Associated Press/Wide World Photos

Pl. 83: © Sam Parrish and United Press International/Corbis-Bettmann

Pls. 87, 95: © Constantine Manos/Magnum Photos

Pl. 91: © James E. Hinton

Pl. 92: © Benedict J. Fernandez, courtesy of the photographer

Pl. 96: © LeRoy W. Henderson, courtesy of the photographer

Pl. 98: © Larry Fink, courtesy of the photographer